Ancestors of Hope Ellen Stewart

Generation 1

1. **Hope Ellen Stewart**, daughter of Robert McDaniel Stewart and Phyllis Olene Tucker was born on 27 Jun 1949 in South Perry, Ohio. She married **David Garland Edwards** on 09 Mar 1968 in Tampa, Florida. He was born on 21 May 1945 in Fort Sumner, New Mexico.

Generation 2

2. **Robert McDaniel Stewart**, son of Van Robert Stewart and Elsie Myrtle Casto was born on 17 Dec 1920 in Mason County, West Virginia. He died on 18 Jul 1977 in Plant City, Florida. He married **Phyllis Olene Tucker**, daughter of William Edward Tucker and Mary Ann Davis on 27 Sep 1940 in Logan, Hocking County, Ohio.

3. **Phyllis Olene Tucker**, daughter of William Edward Tucker and Mary Ann Davis was born on 21 Mar 1922 in Columbus, Ohio. She died on 07 Mar 1991 in Lancaster, Ohio.

More About Robert McDaniel Stewart:
Burial: 21 Jul 1977 in Pleasant Grove Cemetery, Durant, Florida Living In: 1935 Toledo, Lucas County, Ohio
Occupation: 1938 in Hocking County, Ohio; Working in Electrical Refrigeration
Occupation: Apr 1940 in Logan, Hocking County, Ohio; Cab Driver for Cab Company
Occupation: Sep 1940 in South Perry, Hocking County, Ohio; Bar Tender

More About Phyllis Olene Tucker:
Burial: 11 Mar 1991 in New Fairview Cemetery, Logan, Ohio

Phyllis Olene Tucker and Robert McDaniel Stewart had the following children:

    i.   Mary Sandra Stewart, daughter of Robert McDaniel Stewart and Phyllis Olene Tucker was born on 17 Nov 1942 in Columbus, Ohio. She married Harry Davenport. She married Harold Oates.

    ii.   Evlyn Marie Stewart, daughter of Robert McDaniel Stewart and Phyllis Olene Tucker was born on 17 Dec 1944 in South Perry, Ohio. She married Franklin Eugene Timms. He was born on 03 May 1940 in Dundas, Ohio.

    iii. Jon Robert Stewart, son of Robert McDaniel Stewart and Phyllis Olene Tucker was born on 15 Dec 1947 in Logan, Ohio. He died on 17 Dec 1947 in Logan, Ohio.

       More About Jon Robert Stewart:
       Burial: 18 Dec 1947 in Smith Chapel Cemetery, Logan, Hocking County, Ohio Cause Of Death: Premature

       Notes for Jon Robert Stewart: Buried with his paternal grandparents.

2.   iv. Hope Ellen Stewart, daughter of Robert McDaniel Stewart and Phyllis Olene Tucker was born on 27 Jun 1949 in South Perry, Ohio. She married David Garland Edwards on 09 Mar 1968 in Tampa, Florida. He was born on 21 May 1945 in Fort Sumner, New Mexico.

Generation 3

4. **Van Robert Stewart**, son of Henry W. Stewart and Deborah McDaniel was born on 01 Sep 1863 in Mason County, West Virginia. He died on 07 Nov 1939 in Falls Township, Hocking County, Ohio.

He married **Elsie Myrtle Casto**, daughter of George Washington Casto and Margaret Frances Johnston on 28 May 1910 in Gallia County, Ohio.

5.   **Elsie Myrtle Casto**, daughter of George Washington Casto and Margaret Frances Johnston was born on 15 Jun 1893 in Jackson County, West Virginia. She died on 09 Nov 1957 in Ohio.

More About Van Robert Stewart:
Burial: 10 Nov 1939 in Smith Chapel Cemetery, Logan, Hocking County, Ohio
Occupation: 1900 in Waggener District, Mason County, West Virginia; Day
Labor
Occupation: 1910 in Logan, Hocking County, Ohio; Carpenter in Car Shop
Occupation: 1920 in Green Township, Hocking County, Ohio; Hotel Proprietor
Occupation: 1926 in Toledo, Lucas County, Ohio; Car Repair
Occupation: 1928 in Toledo, Lucas County, Ohio; Laborer
Occupation: 1930 in Toledo, Lucas County, Ohio; Salesman
Occupation: 07 Apr 1930 in Toledo, Lucas County, Ohio; Carpenter for Steam Railroad

Notes for Van Robert Stewart:
• Funeral services were held Friday at 2 o'clock at the Iron Street Church for Van Robert Stewart,76, of West Logan, who was killed Tuesday afternoon on U. S. Route 33 near the state highway barns when he was struck by a truck driven by Delmar Walker, Sugar Grove, employee of Ohio Fuel Gas Co. Rev Glenn Lehman McCuneville was in charge of the services and was assisted by Rev. A.F. Pinell, local pastor. Burial was made at Smith Chapel Cemetery by Heinlein Bros. with Clyde Henry and Floyd Stewart, Miranda Castro, John Thomas and Phillip Devol acting
as pallbearers. Prosecutor Hubert D. Lappen is conducting an investigation as to the accident, which occurred during a drizzling rain.
       published November 10, 1939

More About Elsie Myrtle Casto:
Burial: 12 Nov 1957 in Smith Chapel Cemetery, Logan, Hocking County, Ohio
Living In: 1940 Falls Township, Hocking County, Ohio
Occupation: 1920; Hotel Cook, Hocking County, Ohio

Notes for Elsie Myrtle
Casto:
FUNERAL NOTICE
The Athens Messenger, Athens, Athens County, Ohio, Wednesday 13 Nov 1957

Mrs. Stewarts Rites Are Held Tuesday
LOGAN-Funeral services Myrtle Stewart, 64, widow of the Rev. Van R. Stewart, were held at 2 p.m. Tuesday in the Apostolic Gospel Tabernacle.

The Rev. Edwards officiated and music was furnished by Mrs. Kathleen Wells and Mrs. Leona Harden, accompanied by Miss Shirley Sudlow.

Pallbearers were Merl Huffines, Charles Hurst Jr., Larry Yates, David Baker, Harry Casto, and Lawrence Casto. Burial was made in Smith's Chapel Cemetery by the Heinlein funeral home.

Elsie Myrtle Casto and Van Robert Stewart had the following children:
     i.   Cora Beatrice Stewart, daughter of Van Robert Stewart and Elsie Myrtle Casto was born on 31 Dec 1912 in Logan, Ohio. She died on 21 Jan 2003 in Lancaster, Ohio. She married Lucius Oakley Hartmann, son of Henry Andrew Hartmann and Barbara M. Bort on 07 Mar 1942. He was born on 05 May 1907 in Logan, Hocking County, Ohio. He died on 04 Nov 2000 in Lancaster, Ohio. She married Roy Martin Wood, son of Roy C. Wood and Elizabeth Martin on 16 Oct 1930 in Lucas County, Ohio.

He was born on 20 Apr 1900 in Antioch, Lake County, Illinois. He died on 13
Nov 1984 in Washington County, Florida.

More About Cora Beatrice Stewart:
Burial: 25 Jan 2003 in Maple Grove Cemetery, Lancaster, Fairfield County,
Ohio
Living In: 1935 Athens, Athens County, Ohio
Living In: 1940 Cora and her two children are living with her mother in Falls
Township, Hocking County, Ohio.
Living In: 2003 Lancaster, Ohio
Occupation: 1930 in Toledo, Lucas County, Ohio; Restaurant Waitress
Occupation: 1940 in Falls Township, Hocking County, Ohio; Working in
Shoe Factory

More About Lucius Oakley Hartmann:
Living In: 1920 Hocking County, Ohio
Living In: 1930 With his mother in Lancaster, Fairfield County, Ohio
Living In: 1940 With his mother and step father in Lancaster, Fairfield County,
Ohio.
Occupation: 1930 in Lancaster, Fairfield County, Ohio; Fore-Boy in Glass Factory
Occupation: 1940 in Lancaster, Fairfield County, Ohio; Tumble Department in
Glass Factory

More About Roy Martin Wood:
Burial: Glenwood Cemetery, Chipley, Washington County, Florida
Occupation: 1946 in Franklin County, Ohio; Refrigeration Engineer

ii.   Lillian G. Stewart, daughter of Van Robert Stewart and Elsie Myrtle Casto was
       born on 06 Mar 1916 in Logan, Hocking County, Ohio. She died on 06 Jan 2000
       in Sylvania, Lucas County, Ohio. She married Paul E. Uncle. He was born on 31
       Dec 1910 in Perkins Township, Erie County, Ohio. He died on 20 Feb 1984 in
       Toledo, Lucas County, Ohio. She married Jack Wade.

       More About Lillian G. Stewart:
       Burial: 10 Jan 2000 in Ottawa Hills Memorial Park, Toledo, Lucas County,
       Ohio
       Living In: 2000 Toledo, Ohio
       Occupation: Toledo, Lucas County, Ohio; Worked 18 years as a Punch Operator
       for Toledo Die and Manufacturing

       Notes   for   Lillian   G.
       Stewart: No Children.

       More About Paul E. Uncle:
       Burial: 24 Feb 1984 in Ottawa Hills Memorial Park, Toledo, Lucas County,
       Ohio
       Living In: 1984 Toledo, Ohio
       Occupation: 1932 in Detroit Michigan; Butcher
       Occupation: 1940 in Toledo, Lucas County, Ohio; Truck Driver for Wholesale
       Fruit Dealer
       Military Service: Bet. 13 May 1942-05 Dec 1945 Entered Service at Camp Perry,
       Ohio; U.S Army, World War Two

       Notes for Paul E. Uncle:

Retired in 1971 as a truck driver for Suburban Freight Company after 32 years service.

Lucas County, Ohio deputy Sheriff in 1950's.

Candidate for Lucas County, Ohio sheriff in 1968.

Served in Europe during World War Two. Awarded Purple Heart and Bronze Star.
----

    iii.   Marie D. Stewart, daughter of Van Robert Stewart and Elsie Myrtle Casto was born on 04 Sep 1918 in Logan, Ohio. She died on 05 Mar 1940 in Falls Township, Hocking County, Ohio. She married Arthur B. Hilt. He was born on 16 May 1916 in Hocking County, Ohio. He died on 07 Jun 1963 in Nelsonville, Athens County, Ohio.

More About Marie D. Stewart:
Burial: 08 Mar 1940 in Smith Chapel Cemetery, Logan, Hocking County, Ohio Cause Of Death: Pulmonary Tuberculosis

More About Arthur B. Hilt:
Burial: Greenlawn Cemetery, Nelsonville, Athens County, Ohio
Living In: 1935 Nelsonville, Athens County, Ohio
Living In: 1940 With his sister, Sylvia, and her family in York Township, Athens County, Ohio.
Living In: 1963 Nelsonville, Athens County, Ohio
Occupation: 1940 in York Township, Athens County, Ohio; W.P.A. Laborer
Military Service: 02 Jul 1945 Enlisted in U. S. Army at Fort Hayes, Columbus, Franklin County, Ohio; Private, Company E, 1560th Service Command Unit, World War Two

2.   iv. Robert McDaniel Stewart, son of Van Robert Stewart and Elsie Myrtle Casto was born on 17 Dec 1920 in Mason County, West Virginia. He died on 18 Jul 1977 in Plant City, Florida. He married Phyllis Olene Tucker, daughter of William Edward Tucker and Mary Ann Davis on 27 Sep 1940 in Logan, Hocking County, Ohio. She was born on 21 Mar 1922 in Columbus, Ohio. She died on 07 Mar 1991 in Lancaster, Ohio. He married Opal Mae Ankrom, daughter of Zennie Ankrom and Ethel Hanlin on 14 Feb 1938 in Hocking County, Ohio. She was born on 21 Sep 1920 in Logan, Ohio. She died on 23 Oct 1990 in Circleville, Pickaway County, Ohio.

    v.   William Evert Stewart, son of Van Robert Stewart and Elsie Myrtle Casto was born on 24 Oct 1923 in Hocking County, Ohio. He died on 17 Jan 2009 in Arizona. He married Loretta Jaques, daughter of John Jaques and Retha Nuckles on 26 Nov 1942 in Lucas County, Ohio. She was born on 26 Feb 1925 in Ohio. She died on 15 Dec 1999 in Arizona.

More About William Evert Stewart:
Living In: 2009 Tucson, Pima County, Arizona

More About Loretta Jaques:

vi.   Rolland Richard Stewart, son of Van Robert Stewart and Elsie Myrtle Casto was born on 05 Jan 1926 in Ohio. He died on 19 Jan 2005 in Westerville, Delaware County, Ohio. He married Mary Lou Kessler. She was born on 22 May 1927 in Lancaster, Ohio.

More About Rolland Richard Stewart:
Burial: Resurrection Cemetery, Lewis Center, Delaware County, Ohio
Occupation: 1953 in Columbus, Ohio; Shipping Clerk for Columbus Auto
Parts Military Service: U.S. Navy, World War Two

vii.   Frances Winnifred Stewart, daughter of Van Robert Stewart and Elsie Myrtle Casto was born after 1929 in Ohio. She married Fred R. Hoey. He was born on 10 Nov 1926 in Ohio. He died on 07 Apr 1987 in Wauseon, Fulton County, Ohio. She married Raymond Paul Brescol after 07 Apr 1987. He was born in Ohio.

More About Fred R. Hoey:
Burial: 10 Apr 1987 in Ottawa Hills Memorial Park, Toledo, Lucas County, Ohio Living In: 1987 Delta, Fulton County, Ohio
Military Service: U. S. Navy, World War Two

Notes for Fred R. Hoey:
Worked 37 years as a truck driver for Toledo Edison Company until becoming disabled in 1984.

6.   **William Edward Tucker**, son of Hollis Clark Tucker and Clara Fox was born on 08 Nov 1885 in Rockbridge, Ohio. He died on 21 Apr 1975 in Plant City, Florida. He married **Mary Ann Davis**, daughter of Levi Davis and Mary Ann Bigham on 29 Jun 1906 in Lancaster, Ohio.

7.   **Mary Ann Davis**, daughter of Levi Davis and Mary Ann Bigham was born on 16 Mar 1887 in Laurel Township, Hocking County, Ohio. She died on 11 Mar 1971 in Lakeland, Polk County, Florida.

More About William Edward Tucker:
Burial: Pleasant Grove Cemetery, Durant, Florida
Living In: 1908 Rockbridge, Goodhope Township, Hocking County, Ohio
Living In: 1910 Good Hope Township, Hocking County, Ohio
Occupation: 1920 in Columbus, Franklin County, Ohio; Structural Iron Worker on Bridge Work
Occupation: 1930 in Columbus, Franklin County, Ohio; Iron Worker Building Bridges
Occupation: 1940 in Columbus, Franklin County, Ohio; Iron Worker with Iron Contractor

Notes for William Edward Tucker:
Working as a Union Iron Worker at Jackson Iron and Steel Company, Jackson, Ohio in 1942.

More About Mary Ann Davis:
Burial: Pleasant Grove Cemetery, Durant, Florida
Occupation: School Teacher

Mary Ann Davis and William Edward Tucker had the following children:

i. William Hollis Tucker, son of William Edward Tucker and Mary Ann Davis was born on 28 Jan 1907 in Good Hope Township, Hocking County, Ohio. He died on 13 May 1951 in Nelsonville, Ohio. He married Mazie Ellen Turbett, daughter of Charles Monroe Turbett and Cora Bell Bartley on 02 May 1931 in Franklin County, Ohio. She was born on 10 Feb 1910 in Columbus, Franklin County, Ohio. She died on 11 Jan 1996 in Pickaway County, Ohio.

More About William Hollis Tucker:
Burial: 16 May 1951 in Mount Olive Cemetery, South Perry, Hocking County, Ohio
Cause Of Death: Coronary Thrombosis
Living In: 1930 With his parents in Columbus, Franklin County, Ohio.
Occupation: 1930 in Columbus, Franklin County, Ohio; Iron Worker Building Bridges
Occupation:1931 in Franklin County, Ohio; Painter
Occupation: Magician
Military Service: Company D, 29th Engineer Battalion, U.S. Army, World War Two

More About Mazie Ellen Turbett:
Burial: Mount Olive Cemetery, South Perry, Hocking County, Ohio

ii. Evlyn Marie Tucker, daughter of William Edward Tucker and Mary Ann Davis was born on 18 Jul 1908 in Millville, Hocking County, Ohio. She died on 19 Mar 1988 in Athens, Athens County, Ohio. She married Arthur B. Hilt. He was born on 16 May 1916 in Hocking County, Ohio. He died on 07 Jun 1963 in Nelsonville, Athens County, Ohio. She married Earl Charles Saltz, son of Charles Saltz and Laura Yearling on 15 Jun 1931 in Franklin County, Ohio. He was born on 15 Feb 1899 in Columbus, Franklin County, Ohio. He died on 14 May 1971 in Big Spring, Howard County, Texas.

More About Evlyn Marie Tucker:
Burial: Pleasant Grove Cemetery, Durant, Florida
Living In: 1930 With her parents in Columbus, Franklin County, Ohio.
Living In: 1988 Vinton County, Ohio
Occupation: 1930 in Columbus, Franklin County, Ohio; Cutter in Shoe Factory
Military Service: Bet. 29 Aug 1944-10 Jan 1945 Enlisted July 31, 1944 at Fort Hayes, Columbus, Ohio; U. S. Army, World War Two

Notes   for   Evlyn   Marie Tucker: No Children.

Enlisted in Womens Army Corps at Fort Hayes, Columbus, Ohio on July 31, 1944. Reported for active duty August 29, 1944 at Cleveland, Ohio. Service number A 512 088.

More About Arthur B. Hilt:

Burial: Greenlawn Cemetery, Nelsonville, Athens County,
Ohio
Living In: 1935 Nelsonville, Athens County, Ohio
Living In: 1940 With his sister, Sylvia, and her family in York Township, Athens
County, Ohio.
Living In: 1963 Nelsonville, Athens County, Ohio
Occupation: 1940 in York Township, Athens County, Ohio; W.P.A. Laborer
Military Service: 02 Jul 1945 in Enlisted in U. S. Army at Fort Hayes, Columbus,
Franklin County, Ohio; Private, Company E, 1560th Service Command Unit,
World War Two

More About Earl Charles Saltz:
Occupation: 1931 in Columbus, Franklin County, Ohio; Machinist

3.   iii. Phyllis Olene Tucker, daughter of William Edward Tucker and Mary Ann Davis was born
on 21 Mar 1922 in Columbus, Ohio. She died on 07 Mar 1991 in Lancaster, Ohio.
She married Robert McDaniel Stewart, son of Van Robert Stewart and Elsie Myrtle
Casto on 27 Sep 1940 in Logan, Hocking County, Ohio. He was born on 17 Dec 1920
in Mason County, West Virginia. He died on 18 Jul 1977 in Plant City, Florida.

Generation 4

8.   **Henry W. Stewart**, son of William Stewart and Martha Ann Van Sickle was born on 16 Dec 1830
in Mason County, Virginia. He died on 30 Aug 1905 in West Columbia, Mason County, West
Virginia. He married **Deborah McDaniel**, daughter of Hutchinson McDaniel and Hannah Johnson
on 15 Sep 1862 in Point Pleasant, Mason County, Virginia.

9.   **Deborah McDaniel**, daughter of Hutchinson McDaniel and Hannah Johnson was born on 30
Jul 1843 in Mason County, Virginia. She died on 17 Mar 1900 in Mason County, West Virginia.

More About Henry W. Stewart:
Burial: 02 Sep 1905 in Stewart Cemetery, Mason County, West
Virginia
Cause Of Death: Brights Disease
Living In: 1860 With his parents in District 1, Mason County, Virginia
Occupation: 1860 in District 1, Mason County, Virginia; Farmer
Occupation: 1870 in Cuivre Township, Pike County, Missouri; Farmer
Occupation: 1880 in Cuivre Township, Pike County, Missouri; Farmer
Occupation: 1900 in Robinson District, Mason County, West Virginia; Farmer

More About Deborah McDaniel:
Burial: Stewart Cemetery, Mason County, West Virginia

Deborah McDaniel and Henry W. Stewart had the following children:
4.   i. Van Robert Stewart, son of Henry W. Stewart and Deborah McDaniel was born on 01 Sep
1863 in Mason County, West Virginia. He died on 07 Nov 1939 in Falls Township,
Hocking County, Ohio. He married Elsie Myrtle Casto, daughter of George Washington
Casto and Margaret Frances Johnston on 28 May 1910 in Gallia County, Ohio. She
was born on 15 Jun 1893 in Jackson County, West Virginia. She died on 09 Nov 1957
in Ohio. He married Cora B. Swan, daughter of A
. Swan on 24 Oct 1889 in Pike County, Missouri. She was born about 1871 in
Missouri. She died on 28 Dec 1896 in Lincoln County, Missouri. He married Mary
Weber on 08 Aug 1897 in Lincoln County, Missouri. She died before 07 Jun 1900.
      ii. Andrew Johnson Stewart, son of Henry W. Stewart and Deborah McDaniel
was born on 09 Jan 1866 in Mason County, West Virginia.

iii.   William Hudson Stewart, son of Henry W. Stewart and Deborah McDaniel was born on 26 Feb 1868 in Calumet Township, Pike County, Missouri. He died on 18 Jul 1915 in Calumet Township, Pike County, Missouri. He married Martha Ellen Stilffler on 10 Mar 1889 in Ashley Township, Pike County, Missouri. She was born on 28 May 1873 in Wisconsin. She died on 22 Oct 1948 in Elsberry, Lincoln County, Missouri.

More About William Hudson Stewart:
Burial: 19 Jul 1915 in Oak Ridge Cemetery, Lincoln County, Missouri
Cause Of Death: Hit by falling scaffold.
Occupation: 1900 in Buffalo Township, Pike County, Missouri; Day Laborer
Occupation: 1910 in Hurricane Township, Lincoln County, Missouri; Farm Laborer

Notes for William Hudson Stewart:
Death Certificate gives place of death as Calumet Township, Pike County, Missouri.

Injury leading to his death occured in Dameron, Lincoln County, Missouri.

More About Martha Ellen Stilffler:
Burial: 24 Oct 1948 in Elsberry, Lincoln County, Missouri Cause Of Death: Pneumonia
Occupation: 1930 in Cuivre Township, Pike County, Missouri; Laundress at Home

Notes for Martha Ellen Stilffler:
Name used on Marriage license with William Hudson Stewart is Martha Stilffler. Name of her father on her death certificate is Henry Stillpflue, born in Germany.
----

iv.   Viola B. Stewart, daughter of Henry W. Stewart and Deborah McDaniel was born on 25 Dec 1869 in Missouri. She died on 17 Jun 1959 in Clifton, Mason County, West Virginia. She married John Leonard Webber before 27 Apr 1893 in Missouri. He was born on 16 May 1858. He died on 27 Jan 1941. She married George Hamilton Stewart, son of Jesse Franklin Stewart and Sarah Catherine Johnson on 28 May 1900 in New Cumberland, Hancock County, West Virginia. He was born on 27 Dec 1875 in Mason County, West Virginia. He died on 27 Sep 1945 in Athens, Athens County, Ohio.

More About Viola B. Stewart:
Burial: 20 Jun 1959 in Letart Falls Cemetery, Letart Falls, Meigs County, Ohio
Cause Of Death: Bronchial Pneumonia

More About George Hamilton Stewart:
Burial: 01 Oct 1945 in Letart Falls Cemetery, Letart Falls, Meigs County, Ohio Cause Of Death: Chronic Pulmonary Tuberculosis
Occupation: 1904 in Mason County, West Virginia; Laborer
Occupation: 1910 in West Columbia, Mason County, West Virginia; Laborer in Car Shops
Occupation: 1918 in West Columbia, Mason County, West Virginia; Miner
Occupation: 1920 in Waggener District, Mason County, West Virginia ; Miner

Occupation: 1930 in Toronto, Jefferson County, Ohio; Construction Laborer
Occupation: 1940 in Racine, Meigs County, Ohio; No Occupation Listed on
U.S. Census Form

v.   Alveretta Stewart, daughter of Henry W. Stewart and Deborah McDaniel was
born about 1872 in Missouri.

vi.   John Mack Stewart, son of Henry W. Stewart and Deborah McDaniel was born
on 14 Jul 1875 in Pike County, Missouri. He died on 27 Apr 1937 in West
Columbia, Mason County, West Virginia. He married Dora Clementine Lewis,
daughter of Isaac J. Lewis and Elizabeth Wetzel on 18 Oct 1899 in Mason
County, West Virginia. She was born on 09 May 1880 in New Garden Township,
Wayne County, Indiana. She died on 24 Jul 1942 in Charleston, Kanawha
County, West Virginia. He married Elizabeth Rebecca Van Matre, daughter of
David Van Matre and Harriett Rebecca Lewis on 25 Apr 1908 in Hartford, Mason
County, West virginia. She was born on 11 Feb 1889 in West Virginia. She died
on 15 Apr 1979 in Meigs County, Ohio.

More About John Mack Stewart:
Burial: 29 Apr 1937 in Graham Cemetery, Mason County, West
Virginia
Cause Of Death: Polycythemia
Living In: 1900 Living, with his wife Dora, in the household of his father in Mason
County, West Virginia
Occupation: 1900 in Robinson District, Mason County, West Virginia;
Farmer
Occupation: 1910 in Logan, Hocking County, Ohio; Car Carpenter
Occupation: 1920 in Waggener District, Mason County, West Virginia; Car Repair
in Car Shop
Occupation: 1930 in Waggener District, Mason County, West Virginia; Carpenter
in Car Shop

Notes for John Mack Stewart:
World War One draft registration and death certificate have his middle name
as "Mack".

More About Dora Clementine Lewis:
Burial: 26 Jul 1942 in Sattes Cemetery, Charleston, Kanawha County, West
Virginia
Living In: 1910 Divorced and using the name Dora Lewis in Charleston, Kanawha
County, West Virginia.
Living In: 1920 Widowed and using the name Dora Lavin in Peiffer, Kanawha
County, West Virginia
Occupation: 1910 Charleston, Kanawha County, West Virginia; Private Family
Cook for Henrietta Lowenstein and familly.
Occupation: 1920 in Peiffer, Kanawha County, West Virginia; Sewing Seamstress

More About Elizabeth Rebecca Van Matre:
Burial: Graham Cemetery, Mason County, West Virginia
Living In: 1940 Living, with her children Paul and Mary, in Waggener District,
Mason County, West Virginia.

vii.   Henry Egbert Stewart, son of Henry W. Stewart and Deborah McDaniel was born
on 15 Nov 1878 in West Columbia, Mason County, West Virginia. He died on 21

Jan 1951 in Gallipolis, Gallia County, Ohio. He married Eva Louella Thompson, daughter of Green Thompson and Sarah Crookham on 26 Sep 1906 in Clifton, Mason County, West Virginia. She was born on 01 Jun 1886 in West Virginia. She died on 16 Aug 1957 in West Columbia, Mason County, West Virginia.

More About Henry Egbert Stewart:
Burial: 24 Jan 1951 in Suncrest Cemetery, Point Pleasant, Mason County, West Virginia
Cause Of Death: Myocardial Infarction
Living In: 1900 With his brother, Van R. Stewart, in Waggener District, Mason County, West Virginia.
Living In: 1918 West Columbia, Mason County, West Virginia
Living In: 1942 West Columbia, Mason County, West Virginia
Occupation: 1910 in West Columbia, Mason County, West Virginia; Coal Miner
Occupation: 1918 in Hebron, Ohio; Car Carpenter for K.M. Railroad
Occupation: 1920 in Waggener District, Mason County, West Virginia; House Carpenter
Occupation: 1930 in Waggener District, Mason County, West Virginia; Carpenter in Car Factory
Occupation: 1940 in Letart Township, Meigs County, Ohio; Farm Labor
Occupation: 1942 in Middleport, Meigs County, Ohio; Working for N.Y.C. Railroad
Occupation: Truck Gardening

Notes for Henry Egbert Stewart:
Lived in West Columbia, Mason county, West Virginia at the time of his death. Died in Gallipolis, Ohio while in Holzer hospital.

World War One and World War Two draft registrations give date of birth as November 15, 1878. Death certificate and headstone have year of birth as 1877.

More About Eva Louella Thompson:
Burial: 18 Aug 1957 in Suncrest Cemetery, Point Pleasant, Mason County, West Virginia
Cause Of Death: Cerebral Hemorrhage

Notes for Eva Louella Thompson:
Headstone gives year of birth as 1884.

More About Henry Egbert Stewart and Eva Louella Thompson:
Marriage Fact: Married by Reverend Homer J. Metheny
Marriage Fact: Married in United Episcopal Church

viii.	Clyde Wyatt Stewart, son of Henry W. Stewart and Deborah McDaniel was born on 19 Jul 1881 in Pike County, Missouri. He died on 13 Jul 1969 in Clifton, Mason County, West Virginia. He married Martha (Mattie) A. Kearns, daughter of Jesse Kearns and Martha M. Stewart on 11 Jun 1902 in Mason County, West Virginia. She was born on 04 Jun 1885 in Mason County, West Virginia. She died on 06 Nov 1919 in West Columbia, Mason County, West Virginia. He married Anna Lee Rodgers, daughter of John Michael Rodgers and Elizabeth Francis Stewart on 18

Sep 1920 in Point Pleasant, Mason County, West Virginia. She was born on 12 May 1895 in Old Town, Mason County, West Virginia. He married Catherine Virginia Van Meter, daughter of Winfield Scott Van Meter and Margaret May Russell on 02 May 1945 in Gallia County, Ohio. She was born on 23 Jan 1884 in West Columbia, Mason County, Ohio. She died on 17 Aug 1966 in Middleport, Meigs County, Ohio.

More About Clyde Wyatt Stewart:
Burial: 16 Jul 1969 in Riverview Cemetery, Middleport, Meigs County,
Ohio Cause Of Death: Coronary Occlusion and Pulmonary Tuberculosis
Living In: 1918 West Columbia, Mason County, West Virginia
Living In: 1942 Middleport, Meigs County, Ohio
Occupation: 1910 in Logan, Hocking County, Ohio; Car Carpenter
Occupation: 1918 in Hobson, Meigs County, Ohio; Car Carpenter for H.M. Railroad
Occupation: 1920 in Waggener District, Mason County, West Virginia; Car Repairer at Car Works
Occupation: 1930 in Waggener District, Mason County, West Virginia; Car Repairer at Railroad Shop
Occupation: 1942 in Hobson, Meigs County, Ohio; Working for New York Central Railroad
Occupation: 1945 in Middleport, Ohio;
Welder

Notes for Clyde Wyatt Stewart:

CLIFTON - Clyde W. Stewart, 87, Clifton, died early Sunday at a home of a sister, Mrs. Maude Vanmeter, Clifton.

Born in Missouri, he was a son of the late Henry and Deborah McDaniel Stewart.

Surviving are three daughters, Mrs. Mabel Hutton, West Jefferson, Ohio, Mrs. Irene Wells, Pomeroy, and Mrs. Violet Ray, Columbus, Ga.; three sons, Floyd and Almo Stewart, both of Toledo, and Leo of West Columbia; seven stepsons, Tommy, Lonnie, John, Marvin and Clayton Smith and Franklin and Edgar Workman; two sisters, Mrs. Maude VanMeter, Clifton and Mrs. Julia VanMeter, West Columbia.

Funeral services will be held Wednesday at 3 p.m. in West Columbia United Methodist Church with the Rev. O.H. Carder and the Rev. Eddie Boyer officiating. Burial will be in Riverview Cemetery in Middleport.

Friends may call at Foglesong Funeral Home Tuesday 2 to 4 p.m. and 7 to 9 p.m. The body will be taken to the church one hour before the funeral.

Athens Messenger
July 14, 1969.

Middle name is from World War Two draft registration.

More About Martha (Mattie) A. Kearns:
Burial: 08 Nov 1919 in West Columbia, West Virginia
Cause Of Death: Apoplexy

Notes for Anna Lee Rodgers:
Had a twin brother named "Amidei".

More About Catherine Virginia Van Meter:
Burial: Riverview Cemetery, Middleport, Meigs County, ohio

Notes for Catherine Virginia Van Meter:

MIDDLEPORT - Mrs. Catherine Virginia Stewart, 82, 684 Beech Street,
died unexpectedly Wednesday of an apparent heart attack.

Born in Clifton, Jan. 23, 1884, she was the daughter of the late Winfield
and Margaret Russell VanMeter.

Surviving are her husband, Clyde W. Stewart; five sons, Tommy Smith,
Vancroft, W.Va., Lonnie Smith, Chillicothe, John Smith, Nitro, Marvin Smith,
Hometown, W.Va., and Clayton Smith, Cleveland; three stepsons, Floyd and
Almo Stewart, Toledo, and Leo Stewart, West Columbia; three stepdaughters,
Mrs. Tom Wells, Harrisonville, Mrs. Mabelle Hutton, Columbus, and Mrs. Violet
Ray, Phoenix City, Ala.

Also surviving are two brothers, Okey VanMeter, Mason, and Lonnie
VanMeter, Parkersburg; and two sisters, Mrs. Hattie Kay, Point Pleasant, and
Mrs. Guy Nichols, Parkersburg.

Funeral services will be held Sunday at 3:00 p.m. (DST) in Foglesong
Funeral Home by the Rev. Lester Lane. Burial will be in the Riverview
Cemetery in Middleport.

Friends may call at the funeral home after 7 p.m. Friday.

Athens Messenger
August 18, 1966.

Birth record and both marriage licenses have her first name as "Kate".
----

ix.   Maud B. Stewart, daughter of Henry W. Stewart and Deborah McDaniel was born on
23 Sep 1884 in Pike County, Missouri. She died on 19 Mar 1985 in Clifton, Mason
County, West Virginia. She married George Stewart. He was born in Point Pleasant,
Mason County, West Virginia. She married Harry Daniel Van Meter, son of Leonard
Van Meter and Elizabeth Edwards on 25 Dec 1907 in Clifton, Mason County, West
Virginia. He was born on 07 Jul 1874 in Mason County, West Virginia. He died on 02
May 1946 in Clifton, Mason County, West Virginia.

More About Maud B. Stewart:
Burial: Graham Cemetery, Mason County, West Virginia
Living In: 1900 With her brother, Van R. Stewart, in Waggener District, Mason
County, West Virginia.

Notes for Maud B. Stewart:
Social Security death index gives birth date as September 23, 1883 and spells
first name as Maud. Marriage licence indicates a birth year of 1883. 1900 U.S.
Census gives September 1884 as birth date.
Headstone gives date of birth as September 23, 1884. First name is spelled Maud

when she signs her husband's death certificate. First name is spelled Maud on her husband's World War One draft registration. First name is spelled Maud on her headstone.

More About Harry Daniel Van Meter:
Burial: 06 May 1946 in Graham Cemetery, Mason County, West Virginia
Cause Of Death: Cerebral Thrombosis
Occupation: 1910 in Clifton, Mason County, West Virginia; Coal Miner
Occupation: 1920 in Clifton, Mason County, West Virginia; Railroad Laborer
Occupation: 1923 in Railroad Brakeman
Occupation: 1930 in Clifton, Mason County, West Virginia; Railroad Brakeman
Occupation: 1940 in Clifton, Mason County, West Virginia; Railroad Brakeman

Notes for Harry Daniel Van Meter:
Death Certificate (Maud is informant) gives date of birth as July 7, 1874. World War One draft registration gives date of birth as July 17, 1875. 1880 U.S. census indicates a birth year of 1875. Headstone has year of birth as 1874.

----

x.   Julia F. Stewart, daughter of Henry W. Stewart and Deborah McDaniel was born on
        3 Jan 1887 in Pike County, Missouri. She died in May 1972 in Mason County, West
        Virginia. She married Howard D. Van Matre, son of David Van Matre and Harriett
        Rebecca Lewis on 26 Aug 1905 in Point Pleasant, Mason County, West Virginia. He
        was born on 17 Aug 1883 in Mason County, West Virginia. He died on
        6 Feb 1957 in West Columbia, Mason County, West Virginia.

        More About Julia F. Stewart:
        Burial: Graham Cemetery, Mason County, West Virginia

        More About Howard D. Van Matre:
        Burial: 08 Feb 1957 in Graham Cemetery, Mason County, West
        Virginia Cause Of Death: Coronary Occlusion
        Occupation: 1910 in West Columbia, Mason County, West Virginia; Coal Miner
        Occupation: 1920 in Waggener District, Mason County, West Virginia; Coal
        Miner
        Occupation: 1930 in Waggener District, Mason County, West Virginia; Laborer
        in Railroad Shop
        Occupation: 1940 in Waggener District, Mason County, West Virginia; Laborer
        in Railroad Shop

10.   **George Washington Casto**, son of George R. Casto and Susanna Dewees was born on 09
        Aug 1847 in Jackson County, Virginia. He died on 13 Nov 1926 in Falls Township, Hocking
        County, Ohio. He married **Margaret Frances Johnston**, daughter of Abraham E. Johnston and
        Susan L. McMillan on 14 Dec 1878 in Mason County, West Virginia.

11.   **Margaret Frances Johnston**, daughter of Abraham E. Johnston and Susan L. McMillan was
        born on 08 Dec 1856 in Grafton, Taylor County, Virginia. She died on 29 Dec 1928 in Marion
        Township, Franklin County, Ohio.

More About George Washington Casto:
Burial: 15 Nov 1926 in Oak Grove Cemetery, Logan, Hocking County, Ohio
Living In: 1870 With his father and step mother in Union Township, Jackson County, West
Virginia.
Occupation: 1870 in Union Township, Jackson County, West Virginia; Farm
Laborer
Occupation: 1880 in Cologne District, Mason County, West Virginia; Farm Laborer
Occupation: 1900 in Ripley District, Jackson County, West Virginia; Farmer
Occupation: 1910 in Logan, Hocking County, Ohio; Odd Jobs Laborer
Occupation: 1920 in Falls Township, Hocking County, Ohio; General Farm Laborer

More About Margaret Frances Johnston:
Burial: 31 Dec 1928 in Oak Grove Cemetery, Logan, Hocking County,
Ohio Cause Of Death: Organic Heart Trouble
Occupation: 1910 in Logan, Hocking County, Ohio; At Home Washerwoman

More About George Washington Casto and Margaret Frances Johnston: Marriage
Fact: Married in the home of the Bride's father by B.A. Armstrong, M.G.

Margaret Frances Johnston and George Washington Casto had the following children:

i.   Cora Belle Casto, daughter of George Washington Casto and Margaret Frances
     Johnston was born on 02 Nov 1879 in Mason County, West Virginia. She died on
     27 Apr 1956 in Jackson County, West Virginia. She married George Wilman
     Lathey, son of Joseph W. Lathey and Emma Ward on 26 Feb 1899 in Center Point
     School House, Jackson County, West Virginia. He was born on 07 May 1878 in
     Meigs County, Ohio. He died on 16 Dec 1945 in Friendly, Pleasants County, West
     Virginia.

     More About Cora Belle Casto:
     Burial: Foster Chapel Cemetery, Evans, Jackson County, West Virginia

     More About George Wilman Lathey:
     Burial: 18 Dec 1945 in Foster Chapel Cemetery, Evans, Jackson County, West
     Virginia
     Cause Of Death: Myocarditis
     Occupation: Farmer

ii. Rosa Ellen Casto, daughter of George Washington Casto and Margaret Frances
     Johnston was born on 28 Aug 1881 in Cottageville, Jackson County, West
     Virginia. She died on 29 Jan 1976 in Mansfield, Richland County, Ohio. She
     married Kelley Freeman Kay, son of John Kay and Catherine (unknown) on 20
     Jan 1901 in Jackson County, West Virginia. He was born on 22 Dec 1877 in
     Jackson County, West Virginia. He died on 30 Oct 1918 in Logan, Hocking
     County, Ohio. She married Frank Elmer Wolfe, son of David Wolfe and Mary
     Mowery on 20 Feb 1926 in Franklin County, ohio. He was born on 19 May 1884 in
     Hocking county, Ohio. He died on 11 Jun 1950 in Cleveland, Cuyahoga County,
     Ohio. She married Albert Burkhart, son of Fred Burkhart and Mary Haggi on 21
     Apr 1939 in Perry County, Ohio. He was born on 30 Jan 1896 in Ohio. He died on
     16 Dec 1968 in Columbus, Franklin County, Ohio.

     More About Rosa Ellen Casto:
     Burial: Oak Grove Cemetery, Logan, Hocking County, Ohio
     Living In: 1976 Last residence was in Logan, Hocking County, Ohio

More About Kelley Freeman Kay:
Burial: 02 Nov 1918 in Oak Grove Cemetery, Logan, Hocking County, Ohio
Cause Of Death: Pleurisy and Heart Disease - contributing cause was
influenza
Occupation: Section Foreman

More About Kelley Freeman Kay and Rosa Ellen Casto:
Marriage Fact: Married in the home of the bride's parents.

More About Frank Elmer Wolfe:
Burial: 13 Jun 1950 in Oak Grove Cemetery, Logan, Hocking County, Ohio

More About Albert Burkhart:
Burial: Oak Grove Cemetery, Logan, Hocking County, Ohio
Living In: 1968 Columbus, Franklin County, Ohio
Military Service: Company C, 50th Engineers, World War One

iii.   Miranda Nicholas Casto, son of George Washington Casto and Margaret Frances
Johnston was born on 09 Aug 1883 in Cottageville, Jackson County, West
Virginia. He died on 27 Jan 1971 in Hocking County, Ohio. He married Bessie
Louesa Ruble, daughter of James Merley Ruble and Mary Jane Poling on 29 Jan
1907 in Hocking County, Ohio. She was born on 03 Jan 1883 in Falls Township,
Hocking County, Ohio. She died in 1955. He married Xema Bray Vest, daughter
of Joseph Vest and Clara M. Bray on 07 Jun 1958 in Hocking County, Ohio. She
was born on 26 Mar 1889 in Benton Township, Hocking County, Ohio. She died
on 10 Apr 1987 in Logan, Hocking County, Ohio.

More About Miranda Nicholas Casto:
Burial: Oak Grove Cemetery, Logan, Hocking County, Ohio
Living In: 1907 Logan, Ohio
Living In: 1942 Logan, Ohio
Living In: 1971 Logan, Ohio
Occupation: 1942 ; Working at Hocking Valley Brick Company
Occupation: Minister

Notes for Miranda Nicholas Casto:
World War One and World War Two draft registrations give middle name
as Nichola.

More About Bessie Louesa Ruble:
Burial: Oak Grove Cemetery, Logan, Hocking County, Ohio

Notes for Bessie Louesa Ruble:
1900 U.S. census gives name as Lulu Ruble.
Marriage certificate gives name as Lulu Ruble.
Birth record gives name as Bessie Louesa
Ruble. Head Stone gives first name as Louise.
Husband's World War Two draft registration gives Louise as first name of wife.

More About Xema Bray Vest:

Burial: Fairview Memorial Gardens, Rockbridge, Hocking County, Ohio

Notes for Xema Bray Vest:
Buried beside her first husband, Harley Clinton Kalklosch.

----

iv. Susan Elpha Casto, daughter of George Washington Casto and Margaret Frances Johnston was born on 27 May 1886 in Jackson County, West Virginia. She married James Darlington Coakley, son of Augustus Coakley and Margaret Joy on 29 May 1903 in Hocking County, Ohio. He was born on 27 Dec 1877 in York Township, Athens County, Ohio. He died on 01 Feb 1954 in Lancaster, Ohio. She married Joseph Edgar Lattimer, son of David Lattimer and Catherine Willison on 30 Dec 1919 in Hocking County, Ohio. He was born on 24 Aug 1890 in Starr Township, Hocking County, Ohio. He died on 07 Mar 1971 in Hocking County, Ohio.

More About James Darlington Coakley:
Burial: Forest Rose Cemetery, Lancaster, Fairfield Count, Ohio

More About James Darlington Coakley and Susan Elpha Casto:
Marriage Fact: Married by Reverend T. B. White

More About Joseph Edgar Lattimer:
Living In: 1971 Logan, Hocking County, Ohio

v.   A. J. Casto, daughter of George Washington Casto and Margaret Frances Johnston was born on 06 Oct 1888 in Jackson County, West Virginia. She died before 16 Jun 1900.

Notes for A. J. Casto:
Birth date and gender are from birth record.

vi. Robert Edward Casto, son of George Washington Casto and Margaret Frances Johnston was born on 03 Mar 1891 in Cologne District, Mason County, West Virginia. He died on 13 Oct 1958 in Columbus, Franklin County, Ohio. He married Mary E. Friend. She was born on 17 Feb 1896 in Groveport, Franklin County, Ohio. She died on 13 Nov 1978 in Columbus, Franklin County, Ohio.

More About Robert Edward Casto:
Burial: Forest Lawn Memorial Gardens, Columbus, Franklin County, Ohio Living In: 1958 Columbus, Franklin County, Ohio
Occupation: 1910 in Logan, Hocking County, Ohio; Odd Jobs Laborer
Occupation: 1930 in Groveport, Franklin County, Ohio; Barber in his own Barber Shop
Occupation: 1942 in Columbus, Franklin County, Ohio; Barber in his own Barber Shop

More About Mary E. Friend:
Burial: Forest Lawn Memorial Gardens, Columbus, Franklin County, Ohio

Living In: 1978 in Columbus, Franklin County, Ohio

Notes for Mary E. Friend:
Birth date of February 17, 1896 is from birth record. Social Security death
index has birth date of February 18, 1896.

5.   vii. Elsie Myrtle Casto, daughter of George Washington Casto and Margaret Frances
              Johnston was born on 15 Jun 1893 in Jackson County, West Virginia. She died on
              9 Nov 1957 in Ohio. She married Van Robert Stewart, son of Henry W. Stewart
              and Deborah McDaniel on 28 May 1910 in Gallia County, Ohio. He was born on
              01 Sep 1863 in Mason County, West Virginia. He died on 07 Nov 1939 in Falls
              Township, Hocking County, Ohio.
         ix. Lestie Gertrude Casto, daughter of George Washington Casto and Margaret Frances
              Johnston was born on 08 Aug 1896 in Jackson County, West Virginia. She married
              James Everett Stewart, son of Van Robert Stewart and Cora B. Swan on
              14 Jun 1913 in Hocking County, Ohio. He was born on 25 Jan 1891 in Silex,
              Lincoln County, Missouri. He died in Oct 1963 in West Virginia. She married
              Abram Barber, son of Jared Barber and Alice H. Walls on 04 Aug 1923 in Franklin
              County, Ohio. He was born on 14 Jul 1895 in Mundy, Hocking County, Ohio. He
              died on 25 Jul 1964 in Nelsonville, Athens County, Ohio.

         More About Lestie Gertrude Casto:
         Living In: 1913 Logan, Hocking County, Ohio
         Living In: 27 Jan 1920 living as Gertrude Casto with Van Robert Stewart and his
         family in Green Township, Hocking County, Ohio.
         Living In: 1923 Franklin County, Ohio
         Occupation: 14 Jun 1913 in Logan, Hocking County, Ohio; Dining Room Girl
         Occupation: 1920 in Green Township, Hocking County, Ohio; Cook in hotel
         Owned by Van Robert Stewart

         More About James Everett
         Stewart: b: 25 Jan 1891
         Burial: Graham Cemetery, Mason County, West Virginia
         Living In: 1935 Letart Township, Meigs County, Ohio
         Living In: 1942 Kaylong, Mason County, West Virginia
         Occupation: 1910 in Logan, Hocking County, Ohio; Railroad Laborer
         Occupation: 14 Jun 1913 in Logan, Hocking County, Ohio; Wire Worker
         Occupation: 1930 in Letart Township, Meigs County, Ohio; Truck Farmer
         Occupation: 1940 in Graham District, Mason County, West Virginia; Farmer
         Occupation: 1942 in Point pleasant, Mason County, West Virginia; Working
         for Marietta Manufacturing Company

         More About Abram Barber:
         Living In: 1964 Hocking County, Ohio
         Occupation: 1923 in Nelsonville, Athens County, Ohio; Miner
         Occupation: 1942 in Cawthorne Coal Company, Nelsonville, Ohio

         Notes for Abram Barber:
         Birth place is from World War Two draft registration.

12. **Hollis Clark Tucker**, son of Wesley Summers Tucker and Phebe Hutson was born on 15 Aug 1858 in Hocking County, Ohio. He died on 25 Apr 1916 in Columbus, Franklin County, Ohio. He married **Clara Fox**, daughter of Peter Fox and Deborah White on 16 Feb 1879 in Hocking County, Ohio.

13. **Clara Fox**, daughter of Peter Fox and Deborah White was born on 27 Sep 1857 in Laurel Township, Hocking County, Ohio. She died on 30 Dec 1923 in Laurelville, Hocking County, Ohio.

More About Hollis Clark Tucker:
Burial: 28 Apr 1916 in Fairview Methodist Church Cemetery, Good Hope Township, Hocking County, Ohio
Cause Of Death: Punctured lung from fractured ribs due to being run down by a railroad train.
Occupation: 1870; Farm Worker, Laurel, Ohio
Occupation: 1900 in Rockbridge, Goodhope Township, Hocking County, Ohio; Derrick Builder
Occupation: 1910 in Goodhope Township, Hocking County, Ohio; Laborer
Occupation: Carpenter

Notes for Hollis Clark Tucker:
Death certificate gives birth date as August 15, 1854. Age given on death certificate would give a birth date of August 15, 1858. 1900 U.S. census gives birthdate as August 1858. Hollis Tucker and Clara Fox marriage license indicates an 1858 birth.

More About Clara Fox:
Burial: 01 Jan 1924 in Mount Olive Cemetery, South Perry, Hocking County,
Ohio Cause Of Death: Broncial Pneumonia

Notes for Clara Fox:
1860 U.S. census has Clarissa for her first name. Her sister, Sarah, had a daughter named Clarissa.

Clara Fox and Hollis Clark Tucker had the following children:
    i.   Charles Joseph Tucker, son of Hollis Clark Tucker and Clara Fox was born on 12 Oct 1879 in Hocking County, Ohio. He died on 13 Jan 1967 in Hocking County, Ohio. He married Beatrice Applegate, daughter of Walter Applegate and Miranda McFarland about 1903. She was born on 08 Mar 1883 in Lancaster, Ohio. She died on 13 Feb 1952 in Hocking County, Ohio.

    More About Charles Joseph Tucker:
Living In: 1900 Living with his paternal grandparents in Rockbridge, Goodhope Township, Hocking County, Ohio
Living In: 1910 Goodhope Township, Hocking County, Ohio
Living In: 1920 Franklin, Franklin County, Ohio
Living In: 193 Columbus, Franklin County, Ohio
Living In: 1940 Columbus, Franklin County, Ohio
Occupation: 1900 in Rockbridge, Good Hope Township, Hocking County, Ohio; Rig Builder

    More About Beatrice Applegate:
Burial: 16 Feb 1952 in Sunset Cemetery, Galloway, Franklin County, Ohio

ii. Mary Lovetta Tucker, daughter of Hollis Clark Tucker and Clara Fox was born on 17 Aug 1883 in Perry Township, Hocking County, Ohio. She died on 17 Feb 1951 in Salt Creek Township, Hocking County, Ohio. She married William Elmer Woltz, son of Moses H. Woltz and Anna L. Shellhammer on 14 Dec 1901 in Logan, Ohio. He was born on 30 Dec 1880 in Good Hope Township, Hocking County, Ohio. He died in 1955.

More About Mary Lovetta Tucker:
Burial: 20 Feb 1951 in Mount Olive Cemetery, South Perry, Hocking County, Ohio Cause Of Death: Coronary Thrombosis

Notes for Mary Lovetta Tucker:
Ohio Marriage Records give Rockbridge, Ohio as birthplace of Mary Tucker.

More About William Elmer Woltz:
Burial: Mount Olive Cemetery, South Perry, Hocking County, Ohio
Living In: 1930 Columbus, Franklin County, Ohio
Living In: 1940 Columbus, Franklin County, Ohio
Occupation: 1900 in Good Hope Township, Hocking County, Ohio; Farm Labor
Occupation: 1910 in Pittsburgh, Allegheny County, Pennsylvania; Stationary Engineer
Occupation: 1920 in Youngstown, Mahoning County, Ohio; Railroad Repairman

Notes for William Elmer Woltz:
World War One draft registration has birth date as November 20, 1881. World War Two draft registration has November 20, 1880 for birth date. 1900 U.S. Census has birth date as November 1883. Marriage license has November 20, 1881 as birth date. Birth record has December 30, 1880 for date of birth.

6.   iii. William Edward Tucker, son of Hollis Clark Tucker and Clara Fox was born on 08 Nov 1885 in Rockbridge, Ohio. He died on 21 Apr 1975 in Plant City, Florida. He married Mary Ann Davis, daughter of Levi Davis and Mary Ann Bigham on 29 Jun 1906 in Lancaster, Ohio. She was born on 16 Mar 1887 in Laurel Township, Hocking County, Ohio. She died on 11 Mar 1971 in Lakeland, Polk County, Florida.

iv. Harry Herbert Tucker, son of Hollis Clark Tucker and Clara Fox was born on 30 Oct 1887 in Good Hope Township, Hocking County, Ohio. He died on 10 Dec 1949 in Kansas. He married Stella May (unknown). She was born on 20 Dec 1892 in Kansas. She died on 23 May 1980.

More About Harry Herbert Tucker:
Burial: Elim Lutheran Cemetery, Marquette, McPherson County, Kansas
Living In: 1917 Kansas City, Missouri
Living In: 1935 Denver, Denver County, Colorado
Living In: 1940 Marquette, McPherson County, Kansas
Occupation: 1917 in Oiler at Interstate Ice Company in Kansas City, Kansas
Occupation: 1920 in Denver, Denver County, Colorado; Machinist in Garage
Occupation: 1930 in Denver, Denver County, Colorado; Commercial Traveler for Farm Implements

14. **Levi Davis**, son of Levi Davis and Mary Ann Rodman was born on 11 May 1839 in Muskingum County, ohio. He died on 08 Apr 1909 in Perry Township, Hocking County, Ohio. He married **Mary Ann Bigham**, daughter of Isaac Bigham and Mary Elizabeth Delong on 10 Mar 1875 in Hocking County, Ohio.

15. **Mary Ann Bigham**, daughter of Isaac Bigham and Mary Elizabeth Delong was born on 15 Feb 1855 in Hocking County, Ohio. She died on 07 Aug 1924 in Greenfield Township, Fairfield County, Ohio.

More About Levi Davis:
Burial: 10 Apr 1909 in Pisqah Church Cemetery, Hocking County, Ohio
Cause Of Death: Bronchial Pneumonia
Living In: 1860 Levi and Mary are living next door to his father in Falls Township, Hocking County, Ohio.
Living In: 1870 Levi and Mary are living next door to her brother, David Shultz, in Hopewell Township, Muskingum County, Ohio.
Occupation: 1860 in Falls Township, Hocking County, Ohio; Farmer
Occupation: 1870 in Hopewell Township, Muskingum County, Ohio; Works on Farm
Occupation: 1880 in Falls Township, Hocking County, Ohio; Minister
Occupation: 1900 in Laurel Township, Hocking County, Ohio; Farmer
Military Service: Bet. 02 Jul 1861-02 May 1862; Company C. 26th Ohio Infantry, U.S. Army

More About Mary Ann Bigham:
Burial: 10 Aug 1924 in Pisgah Church Cemetery, Hocking County, Ohio Cause Of Death: Addisons Disease
Living In: 1924 Lancaster, Fairfield County, Ohio

Mary Ann Bigham and Levi Davis had the following children:

    i.   Levi Davis, son of Levi Davis and Mary Ann Bigham was born on 16 Nov 1875 in Falls Township, Hocking County, Ohio. He died on 13 May 1961 in Hocking County, Ohio. He married Emma Louise Springer, daughter of Edward Springer and Caroline Bailey on 29 Dec 1901 in Hocking County, Ohio. She was born on 25 Feb 1882 in Hocking County, Ohio. She died on 26 Jan 1982 in Circleville, Pickaway County, Ohio.

        More About Levi Davis:
        Burial: Pisgah Church Cemetery, Hocking County, Ohio
        Living In: 1900 With his parents in Laurel Township, Hocking County, Ohio.
        Occupation: 1900 in Laurel Township, Hocking County, Ohio; Day Laborer
        Occupation: 1901 in Rockbridge, Hocking County, Ohio; Saw Mill Hand
        Occupation: 1910 in Perry Township, Hocking County, Ohio; Farmer
        Occupation: 1920 in Laurel Township, Hocking County, Ohio; Farmer
        Occupation: 1930 in Laurel Township, Hocking County, Ohio; Farmer
        Occupation: 1940 in Laurel Township, Hocking County, Ohio; Farmer

        Notes for Levi Davis:

        Never had children.

        Birth record has birth date of November 30, 1875. Marriage license has birth date

of November 16, 1875. World War One draft registration has birth date
of November 16, 1875.

More About Emma Louise Springer:
Burial: Pisgah Church Cemetery, Hocking County, Ohio
Living In: 1982 Hocking County, Ohio

Notes for Emma Louise Springer:
Never had children.

More About Levi Davis and Emma Louise Springer:
Marriage Fact: Married by Rev. J. C. McLaughlin

ii.   Harriett Davis, daughter of Levi Davis and Mary Ann Bigham was born on 05 Apr
         1876 in Laurel Township, Hocking County, Ohio. She died on 20 Aug 1950 in
         Oakland, Alameda County, California. She married Elza Allen Doss on 26 May 1895
         in Pickaway County, Ohio. He was born on 11 Feb 1873 in Crawford County,
         Kansas. He died on 23 Aug 1956 in Oakland, Alameda County, California.

         More About Harriett Davis:
         Burial: Evergreen Cemetery, Oakland, California

         More About Elza Allen Doss:
         Burial: Evergreen Cemetery, Oakland, California
         Occupation: 1900 in Perry Township, Hocking County, Ohio; Farm Labor
         Occupation: 1910 in Hocking Township, Fairfield County, Ohio; Working in
         Shoe Factory
         Occupation: 1920 in Greenfield Township, Fairfield County, Ohio; Farm Laborer
         Occupation: 1930 in Oakland, Alameda County, California; Receiving Clerk in
         Auto Factory
         Occupation: 1940 in Oakland, Alameda County, California; Sweeper at Fisher Body

iii.   Isaac Wesley Davis, son of Levi Davis and Mary Ann Bigham was born on 12
         Jan 1879 in Logan, Ohio. He died on 22 Sep 1900.

         More About Isaac Wesley Davis:
         Burial: Pisgah Church Cemetery, Hocking County, Ohio
         Occupation: 1900 in Laurel Township, Hocking County, Ohio; Day Laborer

iv.   Lycurgus Davis, son of Levi Davis and Mary Ann Bigham was born on 18 Oct 1880 in
         Falls Township, Hocking County, Ohio. He died on 14 Apr 1928 in Columbus,
         Franklin County, Ohio. He married Myrtle Chambers, daughter of Alexander
         Chambers and Ellen C. Lendennen on 29 Apr 1903 in Logan, Hocking County, Ohio.
         She was born on 23 Feb 1880 in Laurel Township, Hocking County, Ohio.

         More About Lycurgus Davis:

Burial: 17 Apr 1928 in Memorial Burial Park
Occupation: 1900 in Laurel Township, Hocking County, Ohio; Day Laborer
Occupation: 1910 in Lancaster, Fairfield County, Ohio; Watchman at Shoe Factory
Occupation: 1918 in Columbus, Franklin County, Ohio; Shoeworker at H.C. Godman Company
Occupation: 1920 in Columbus, Franklin County, Ohio; Laborer at Motor Company
Occupation: 1928 in Columbus, Franklin County, Ohio; Street Car Conductor

Notes for Lycurgus Davis:
Ohio birth index gives first name as Lycusgus and birth date of November 15, 1880. Marriage Record gives birth date as October 18, 1880. World War One draft registration gives birth date as October 18, 1880. Death certificate gives October 18, 1881 as birth date but age in years given on death certificate indicates a birth year of 1880.

Started using "Curtis" for first name at some point in time between 1910 and 1918.

More About Myrtle Chambers:
Burial: Green Lawn Cemetery, Columbus, Ohio
Living In: 1930 Columbus, Franklin County, Ohio

More About Lycurgus Davis and Myrtle Chambers:
Marriage Fact: Married by Rev. E. G. Guartney

    v.   Samuel Bigham Davis, son of Levi Davis and Mary Ann Bigham was born on 07 Dec 1882 in Sunset, Hocking County, Ohio. He died on 19 Dec 1976 in Bucyrus, Crawford County, Ohio. He married Effie E. Gwartney, daughter of Emmet Gwartney and Margaret Williams on 30 Nov 1905 in Lancaster, Ohio. She was born on 25 Apr 1885 in Perry Township, Hocking County, Ohio. She died on 02 Feb 1961 in Columbus, Franklin County, Ohio.

More About Samuel Bigham Davis:
Burial: Amanda Township Cemetery, Amanda, Fairfield County, Ohio Living In: 1976 Fairfield County, Ohio
Occupation: 1900 in Laurel Township, Hocking County, Ohio; Day Laborer
Occupation: 1910 in Lancaster, Fairfield County, Ohio; Street Car Motorman
Occupation: 1920 in Perry Township, Hocking County, Ohio; Farmer
Occupation: 1930 in Hocking Township, Fairfield County, Ohio; Farmer
Occupation: 1940 in Hocking Township, Fairfield County, Ohio; Farmer

More About Effie E. Gwartney:
Burial: Amanda Township Cemetery, Amanda, Fairfield County, Ohio Living In: 1961 Fairfield County, Ohio

   vi.   George H. Davis, son of Levi Davis and Mary Ann Bigham was born in Apr 1884 in Hocking County, Ohio.

More About George H. Davis:
Occupation: 1900 in Laurel Township, Hocking County, Ohio; Farm Laborer

    vii.   Sarah Dell Davis, daughter of Levi Davis and Mary Ann Bigham was born on 24 Dec 1885 in Laurel Township, Hocking County, Ohio. She died on 01 Nov 1957 in Athens, Ohio. She married Daniel Bailey, son of Charles Bailey and Christena Deischle on 28 Dec 1905 in Hocking County, Ohio. He was born on 02 Nov 1875 in Rockbridge, Good Hope Township, Hocking County, Ohio. He died on 20 Dec 1956 in Logan, Ohio.

More About Sarah Dell Davis:
Burial: Union Church Cemetery, Good Hope Township, Hocking County, Ohio

Notes for Sarah Dell Davis:
Marriage Record gives birthplace as Laurel Township, Hocking County, Ohio.

More About Daniel Bailey:
Burial: Union Church Cemetery, Good Hope Township, Hocking County, Ohio
Occupation: 1900 in Good Hope Township, Hocking County, Ohio; Pipe Line Labor
Occupation: 1910 in Good Hope Township, Hocking County, Ohio; Labor on Gas Line
Occupation: 1920 in Good Hope Township, Hocking County, Ohio; Farmer
Occupation: 1930 in Good Hope Township, Hocking County, Ohio; Farm Operator
Occupation: 1940 in Good Hope Township, Hocking County, Ohio; Farmer

Notes for Daniel Bailey:
World War One draft registration has birth date of October 2, 1875. 1900 U.S. census has birth date of November 1875. Headstone has birth year of 1875. Ohio Births has birth date of October 3, 1876.
----

7.   viii.   Mary Ann Davis, daughter of Levi Davis and Mary Ann Bigham was born on 16 Mar 1887 in Laurel Township, Hocking County, Ohio. She died on 11 Mar 1971 in Lakeland, Polk County, Florida. She married William Edward Tucker, son of Hollis Clark Tucker and Clara Fox on 29 Jun 1906 in Lancaster, Ohio. He was born on 08 Nov 1885 in Rockbridge, Ohio. He died on 21 Apr 1975 in Plant City, Florida.

    ix.   Esena Bell Davis, daughter of Levi Davis and Mary Ann Bigham was born on 05 Jun 1889 in Hocking County, Ohio. She died on 15 Jul 1982 in Columbus, Franklin County, Ohio. She married Wilmer Joseph Jackson, son of Joseph Jackson and Ida Bell on 03 Mar 1906. He was born on 14 Aug 1886 in Sugar Grove, Franklin County, Ohio. He died on 18 Sep 1969 in Columbus, Ohio.

More About Esena Bell Davis:
Burial: Forest Lawn Cemetery, Columbus Ohio

More About Wilmer Joseph Jackson:
Burial: Forest Lawn Cemetery, Columbus Ohio
Occupation: 1910 in Greenfield Township, Fairfield County, Ohio; Section Laborer

on Railroad
Occupation: 1917 in Columbus, Franklin County, Ohio; Locomotive Fireman
on Hocking Valley Railroad
Occupation: 1920 in Columbus, Franklin County, Ohio; Engineer on Hocking
Valley Railroad
Occupation: 1930 in Columbus, Franklin County, Ohio; Railroad Mechanic
Occupation: 1941 in Columbus, Franklin County, Ohio; Locomotive Engineer
Occupation: 1942 in Columbus, Franklin County, Ohio; Working on C&O Railroad

  x. Charles Davis, son of Levi Davis and Mary Ann Bigham was born on 10 Jan
1891 in Laurel Township, Hocking County, Ohio. He died on 15 Jan 1891.

More About Charles Davis:
Burial: Pisgah Church Cemetery, Hocking County, Ohio

Notes for Charles Davis:
Cemetery survey gives birth date of December 5, 1890 and death date of
December 10, 1890. Birth record shows birth date of January 10, 1891.
----

  xi. Lyda Jane Davis, daughter of Levi Davis and Mary Ann Bigham was born on 25
Dec 1891 in Laurel Township, Hocking County, Ohio. She died on 25 Nov 1981 in
Lancaster, Fairfield County, Ohio. She married Anthony Shonk, son of Arron
Shonk and Catherine Wohlsheid on 15 Jul 1912. He was born on 14 Jan 1877 in
Madison Township, Fairfield County, Ohio. He died on 20 Oct 1943 in Lancaster,
Fairfield County, Ohio.

More About Lyda Jane Davis:
Burial: St. Mary's Cemetery, Lancaster, Fairfield County, Ohio
Occupation: 1910 in Madison Township, Fairfield County, Ohio; Working as
a servant in the home of Anthony Shonk.

More About Anthony Shonk:
Burial: St. Mary's Cemetery, Lancaster, Fairfield County, Ohio
Living In: 1900 With his parents in Madison Township, Fairfield County, Ohio.
Occupation: 1900 in Madison Township, Fairfield County, Ohio; Farm Laborer
Occupation: 1910 in Madison Township, Fairfield County, Ohio; Farmer
Occupation: 1918 in Lancaster, Fairfield County, Ohio; Farmer
Occupation: 1920 in Madison Township, Fairfield County, Ohio; Farmer
Occupation: 1930 in Madison Township, Fairfield County, Ohio; Farmer
Occupation: 1940 in Madison Township, Fairfield County, Ohio; Farm Operator

  xii. Minnie Davis, daughter of Levi Davis and Mary Ann Bigham was born on 03 Oct
1893 in Hocking County, Ohio. She died on 08 Aug 1894 in Hocking County, Ohio.

More About Minnie Davis:
Burial: Pisgah Church Cemetery, Hocking County, Ohio

  xiii. Nelson B. Davis, son of Levi Davis and Mary Ann Bigham was born on 01 Jul 1895

in Laurel Township, Hocking County, Ohio. He died on 06 Nov 1978 in Fairfield
County, Ohio. He married Helen Carrie Kane, daughter of Salem Kane and
Mattie Wilson on 19 Jul 1919. She was born on 28 Aug 1901 in Hocking County,
Ohio. She died on 01 May 1978 in Lancaster, Fairfield County, Ohio.

More About Nelson B. Davis:
Burial: Floral Hills Memory Gardens, Lancaster, Fairfield County, Ohio
Occupation: 1920 in Hocking Township, Fairfield County, Ohio; House
Carpenter
Occupation: 1930 in Greenfield Township, Fairfield County, Ohio; Contract
Carpenter
Occupation: 1940 in Lancaster, Fairfield County, Ohio; Building Contractor
Occupation: 1942 in Lancaster, Fairfield County, Ohio; Building Contractor
Military Service: Bet. 30 May 1917-21 Apr 1919 in 148th Infantry, U. S. Army;
World War One

Notes for Nelson B. Davis: Headstone
has 1979 for year of death.

Served in Ypres-Lys and Meuse-Argonne sectors with the American
Expeditionary Force in France during World War One.
Served in Company G, 148th Infantry until June 10, 1918. Served in
Medical department 148th Infantry June 10, 1918 until discharge.

More About Helen Carrie Kane:
Burial: Floral Hills Memory Gardens, Lancaster, Fairfield County, Ohio

Generation 5

16. **William Stewart**, son of Robert Stewart and Catherine Aleshire was born on 09 Sep 1802 in
Bath County, Virginia. He died on 16 Jul 1882 in Mason County, West Virginia. He married
Martha Ann Van Sickle, daughter of Anthony Van Sickle and Rebecca Van Meter on 13 Sep
1823 in Mason County, Virginia.

17. **Martha Ann Van Sickle**, daughter of Anthony Van Sickle and Rebecca Van Meter was born on 15
Oct 1804 in Mason County, Virginia. She died on 02 Feb 1877 in Mason County, West Virginia.

More About William Stewart:
Burial: Stewart Cemetery, Mason County, West Virginia
Occupation: 1850 in District 38, Mason County, Virginia; Farmer
Occupation: 1860 in District 1, Mason County, Virginia; Farmer
Occupation: 1870 in Robinson District, Mason County, West Virginia; Farmer
Occupation: 1880 in Robinson District, Mason County, West Virginia; Farmer

More About Martha Ann Van Sickle:
Burial: Stewart Cemetery, Mason County, West Virginia

Notes for Martha Ann Van Sickle:
Headstone has 1875 for year of death.

Martha Ann Van Sickle and William Stewart had the following children:

i.   John B. Stewart, son of William Stewart and Martha Ann Van Sickle was born on 17 Dec 1824 in Mason County, Virginia. He died on 23 Aug 1900 in Mason County, West Virginia. He married Elizabeth M. (unknown) on 30 Mar 1851 in Jefferson County, Kentucky. She was born on 20 Sep 1827 in Indiana. She died on 05 Sep 1890.

More About John B. Stewart:
Burial: Stewart Cemetery, Point Pleasant, West Virginia
Occupation: 1850 in Louisville District 1, Jefferson County, Kentucky; Boatman
Occupation: 1860 in District 1, Mason County, Virginia; Can not read occupation on census form.
Occupation: 1870 in Robinson Township, Mason County, West Virginia; Farmer
Occupation: 1880 in Union District, Mason County, West virginia; Farmer

Notes for John B. Stewart:
John married Elizabeth M. Barbour March 30, 1851 in Jefferson County, Kentucky. In the 1850 U.S. census (August 10, 1850) John Stewart, age 26 and born in Virginia, is living three doors away from James and Elizabeth Barbour in Louisville District 1, Jefferson County, Kentucky. James and Elizabeth are listed as born in Indiana, James age 21 and Elizabeth age 22.

Martha has Kentucky as her place of birth on her death certificate. William F. has Kentucky as his place of birth on his marriage license.

Anthony and Henry have their mothers name as Elizabeth Barbaro and born in Indiana.

More About Elizabeth M. (unknown):
Burial: Stewart Cemetery, Point Pleasant, West Virginia
Cause Of Death: Dropsy

ii.   William Stewart, son of William Stewart and Martha Ann Van Sickle was born in 1825 in Mason County, Virginia. He died in 1864. He married Nancy Jane Rice on 31 Jul 1845 in Mason County, Virginia. She was born about 1828 in Mason County, West Virginia. She died after 11 Jun 1880.

More About William Stewart:
Occupation: 1850 in District 38, Mason County, Virginia; Laborer
Occupation: 1860 in District 1, Mason County, Virginia; Can not read occupation on census form.

More About Nancy Jane Rice:
Living In: 1870 With John, Martha, Charles, Elizabeth and George in Robinson Township, Mason County, West Virginia
Living In: 1880 With George and Jesse in Robinson Township, Mason County, West Virginia.

iii.   Julia Ann Stewart, daughter of William Stewart and Martha Ann Van Sickle was born on 04 Oct 1827 in Point Pleasant, Mason County, Virginia. She died on 26

May 1902 in Old Town, Mason County, West Virginia. She married Peter Fielding Hawkins, son of Alphonso B. Hawkins and Jane Trimble Poage on 21 Jun 1849 in Mason County, Virginia. He was born on 18 Mar 1822 in Point Pleasant, Mason County, Virginia. He died on 31 Jul 1890 in Point Pleasant, Mason County, West Virginia.

More About Julia Ann Stewart:
Burial: Lone Oak Cemetery, Point Pleasant, Mason County, West Virginia
Occupation: 1900 in Robinson District, Mason County, West Virginia; Farmer

More About Peter Fielding Hawkins:
Burial: Lone Oak Cemetery, Point Pleasant, Mason County, West
Virginia Living In: 1863 West Columbia, Mason County, West Virginia
Occupation: 1850 in District 38, Mason County, Virginia; Farmer
Occupation: 1860 in District 1, Mason County, Virginia; Farmer
Occupation: 1870 in Robinson Township, Mason County, West Virginia; Works on Farm
Occupation: 1880 in Robinson Township, Mason County, West Virginia; Laborer
Military Service: Bet. 03 Dec 1863-22 Jun 1865; Company G, 13th West Virginia Infantry, U.S.A.

Notes for Peter Fielding Hawkins:
Enlisted in U.S. Army at West Columbia, Mason County, West Virginia.
Mustered out at Wheeling, West Virginia. Promoted to Corporal July 1, 1864.
----

8.   iv. Henry W. Stewart, son of William Stewart and Martha Ann Van Sickle was born on 16 Dec 1830 in Mason County, Virginia. He died on 30 Aug 1905 in West Columbia, Mason County, West Virginia. He married Deborah McDaniel, daughter of Hutchinson McDaniel and Hannah Johnson on 15 Sep 1862 in Point Pleasant, Mason County, Virginia. She was born on 30 Jul 1843 in Mason County, Virginia. She died on 17 Mar 1900 in Mason County, West Virginia.

v.   Charles Volney Stewart, son of William Stewart and Martha Ann Van Sickle was born on 23 Dec 1832 in Mason County, Virginia. He died on 28 Feb 1914 in Mason County, West Virginia. He married Mary Ann White on 27 Dec 1865 in Gallia County, Ohio. She was born on 21 May 1845 in Virginia. She died on 23 Jan 1917 in Mason County, West Virginia.

More About Charles Volney Stewart:
Burial: Stewart Cemetery, Mason County, West Virginia
Living In: 1860 With his parents in District 1, Mason County, Virginia
Living In: 1910 Charles and Mary are living with their son, George, and his family in West Columbia, Mason County, West Virginia.
Occupation: 1870 in West Columbia, Mason County, West Virginia; Grocer
Occupation: 1880 in Clifton, Mason County, West Virginia; Grocer
Occupation: 1900 in West Columbia, Mason County, West Virginia; No Occupation Listed on U.S. Census Form
Occupation: 1910 in West Columbia, Mason County, West Virginia; School Teacher

Notes for Charles Volney Stewart:
Date of death on head stone looks like February 29, 1914 but 1914 was not a Leap

Year.

More About Mary Ann White:
Burial: Stewart Cemetery, Mason County, West Virginia

vi.   Jesse Franklin Stewart, son of William Stewart and Martha Ann Van Sickle was born on 08 Apr 1835 in Mason County, Virginia. He died on 24 Feb 1910 in Toronto, Jefferson County, Ohio. He married Sarah Catherine Johnson, daughter of David B. Johnson and Jane W. Mulford on 25 Sep 1862 in Meigs County, Ohio. She was born on 23 Jan 1844 in Mason County, Virginia. She died on 18 Jul 1933 in Toronto, Jefferson County, Ohio.

More About Jesse Franklin Stewart:
Burial: Point Pleasant, Mason County, West
Virginia Cause Of Death: Organic Heart Disease
Living In: 1860 With his parents in District 1, Mason County, Virginia
Occupation: 1870 in Robinson Township, Mason County, West Virginia;
Farmer
Occupation: 1880 in Robinson District, Mason County, West Virginia; Farmer
Occupation: 1900 in Toronto, Jefferson County, Ohio; Retired Farmer

More About Sarah Catherine Johnson:
Burial: 21 Jul 1933 in Point Pleasant, Mason County, West Virginia
Living In: 1910 With her son, James, in Toronto, Jefferson County, Ohio
Living In: 1920 With her son, James, in Toronto, Jefferson County, Ohio
Living In: 1930 With her son, Amidee, and his family in Island Creek, Jefferson County, Ohio

vii. Mary M. Stewart, daughter of William Stewart and Martha Ann Van Sickle was born on 26 Oct 1836 in Mason County, Virginia. She died on 17 Jan 1920 in Onawa, Monona County, Iowa. She married James S. Kelly on 30 May 1855. He was born on 26 Jun 1833 in Detroit, Michigan. He died on 06 Oct 1918 in Onawa, Monona County, Iowa.

More About Mary M. Stewart:
Burial: Onawa City Cemetery, Onawa, Monona County, Iowa
Living In: 1860 With her parents in District 1, Mason County, Virginia.
Living In: 1920 Franklin, Monona County, Iowa

More About James S. Kelly:
Burial: 07 Oct 1918 in Onawa City Cemetery, Onawa, Monona County, Iowa
Occupation: 1870 in Robinson Township, Mason County, West Virginia;
Farmer
Occupation: 1880 in Union District, Mason County, West Virginia; Farmer
Occupation: 1910 in Onawa, Monona County, Iowa; Retired

viii. Elizabeth Stewart, daughter of William Stewart and Martha Ann Van Sickle was born on 30 Jan 1839 in Mason County, Virginia. She died on 27 May 1926 in

Robinson District, Mason County, West Virginia. She married William McDaniel, son of Hutchinson McDaniel and Hannah Johnson on 19 Dec 1861 in Pleasant Flats, Mason County, Virginia. He was born on 25 Sep 1839 in Mason County, Virginia. He died between 04 Jun 1870-06 Jun 1900.

More About Elizabeth Stewart:
Burial: 29 May 1926 in Stewart Cemetery, Mason County, West
Virginia
Living In: Dec 1879 Mason County, West Virginia
Living In: 1900 As a widow in Robinson Distict, Mason County, West Virginia.
Living In: 1910 As a widow in Robinson District, Mason County, West Virginia.
Living In: 1920 With her grand daughter, Clara, and her family in Robinson District, Mason County, West Virginia.
Occupation: 1900 in Robinson District, Mason County, West Virginia; Farmer

Notes for Elizabeth Stewart:
Death certificate gives burial place as Stewart Cemetery. Headstone is present in Lone Oak Cemetery.

Elizabeth was present at Madaline's wedding to give permission for Madaline to get married but there is no mention of Madaline's father.

More About William
McDaniel: b: 1839
Occupation: 1870 in Cuivre Township, Pike County, Missouri; Farmer

Notes for William McDaniel:
Probably died in Missouri between June 4, 1870 and December 1, 1879.
----

ix.   Zilphia R. Stewart, daughter of William Stewart and Martha Ann Van Sickle was born on 12 Nov 1840 in Mason County, Virginia. She died on 21 Jan 1930 in Point Pleasant, Mason County, West Virginia. She married Cornelius W. White, son of Carlin F. White and Sarah F. Belcher on 05 Nov 1863 in Mason County, West Virginia. He was born on 01 Nov 1840 in Mercer County, Virginia. He died on 02 Nov 1925 in Point Pleasant, Mason County, West Virginia.

More About Zilphia R. Stewart:
Burial: 24 Jan 1930 in Stewart Cemetery, Mason County, West Virginia

More About Cornelius W. White:
Burial: 02 Nov 1925 in Stewart Cemetery, Mason County, West Virginia
Occupation: 1870 in Robinson Township, Mason County, West Virginia; Works on Farm
Occupation: 1880 in Robinson District, Mason County, West Virginia; Farmer
Occupation: 1900 in Cooper District, Mason County, West Virginia
Occupation: 1910 in Cooper District, Mason County, West Virginia; Farmer
Occupation: 1920 in Cooper District, Mason County, West Virginia; Farmer

x. James Riley Stewart, son of William Stewart and Martha Ann Van Sickle was born about 1845 in Mason County, Virginia. He died in May 1875 in Robinson District, Mason County, West Virginia. He married Agnes E. Van Meter, daughter of John VanMeter and Melitha (unknown) on 11 Nov 1868 in Mason County, West Virginia. She was born in Oct 1843 in Mason County, Virginia. She died between 26 Apr 1910-04 Feb 1920.

More About James Riley Stewart:
Occupation: 1970 in Robinson Township, Mason County, West Virginia; Farmer

More About Agnes E. Van Meter:
Living In: 1880 With her four children in Robinson District, Mason County, West Virginia
Living In: 1900 Owner of Farm in Robinson District, Mason County, West Virginia
Living In: 1910 With her son, Charles, in Robinson District, Mason County, West Virginia.

xi. Joseph Newton Stewart, son of William Stewart and Martha Ann Van Sickle was born on 29 Nov 1846 in Mason County, Virginia. He died on 22 May 1922 in Point Pleasant, Mason County, West Virginia. He married Margaret Ann Johnson, daughter of David B. Johnson and Jane W. Mulford on 29 Sep 1870 in Mason County, West Virginia. She was born on 20 Feb 1849 in Mason County, Virginia. She died on 28 Aug 1934 in Point Pleasant, Mason County, West Virginia.

More About Joseph Newton Stewart:
Burial: 24 May 1922 in Stewart Cemetery, Mason County, West Virginia
Living In: 1870 With his parents in Robinson District, Mason County, West Virginia.
Occupation: 1870 in Robinson District, Mason County, West Virginia; Farm Worker
Occupation: 1880 in Robinson District, Mason County, West Virginia; Farmer
Occupation: 1900 in Robinson District, Mason County, West Virginia; Farm Laborer
Occupation: 1910 in Robinson District, Mason County, West Virginia; Farmer
Occupation: 1920 in Robinson District, Mason County, West Virginia; Farmer

More About Margaret Ann Johnson:
Burial: 30 Aug 1934 in Stewart Cemetery, Mason County, West Virginia
Living In: 1930 Robinson District, Mason County, West Virginia

xii. Sarah J. Stewart, daughter of William Stewart and Martha Ann Van Sickle was born on 15 Apr 1850 in Mason County, Virginia. She died before 1887. She married Gilbert Van Sickle, son of Samuel Van Sickle and Susan (unknown) on 06 Feb 1868 in Mason County, West Virginia. He was born on 30 Mar 1845 in Mason County, West Virginia. He died on 26 Mar 1930 in Point Pleasant, Mason County, West Virginia.

More About Gilbert Van Sickle:
Burial: 28 Mar 1930 in Bethel Church Cemetery, Leon, Mason County, West Virginia
Occupation: 1880 in Robinson District, Mason County, West Virginia; Can not read

occupation on census form.
Occupation: 1900 in Robinson District, Mason County, West Virginia; Farmer
Occupation: 1910 in Robinson District, Mason County, West Virginia; Farmer
Occupation: 1920 in Robinson District, Mason County, West Virginia; Laborer

More About Gilbert Van Sickle and Sarah J. Stewart:
Marriage Fact: Married in the home of the bride's parents.

18.   **Hutchinson McDaniel** was born on 04 Aug 1807 in Virginia. He died on 06 Jan 1875 in
Mason County, West Virginia. He married **Hannah Johnson**, daughter of Robert Johnson
and Anna Greenlee on 23 Mar 1833 in Mason County, Virginia.

19.   **Hannah Johnson**, daughter of Robert Johnson and Anna Greenlee was born in 1818 in
Virginia. She died on 30 Nov 1870 in Mason County, West Virginia.

More About Hutchinson McDaniel:
Burial: Pioneer Cemetery, Point Pleasant, Mason County, West Virginia
Occupation: 1850 in District 38, Mason County, Virginia; Farmer
Occupation: 1860 in District 1, Mason County, Virginia; Farmer
Occupation: 1870 in Point Pleasant, Mason County, West Virginia; Jailor

Hannah Johnson and Hutchinson McDaniel had the following children:
　　i.   Van D. McDaniel, son of Hutchinson McDaniel and Hannah Johnson was born
about 1836 in Virginia. He died on 10 Sep 1863 in Point Pleasant, West Virginia.
He married Frances E. Ball, daughter of Thomas Ball and Julia Hogg on 21 Feb
1859 in Mason County, Virginia. She was born in 1839 in Virginia. She died in
1916 in West Virginia.

More About Van D. McDaniel:
Burial: Pioneer Cemetery, Point Pleasant, Mason County, West
Virginia Cause Of Death: Camp Dysentery
Military Service: Bet. 09 Oct 1862-10 Sep 1863 in Company C, 13th West
Virginia Infantry, U.S. Army

Notes for Van D. McDaniel:
Died of disease while serving in U.S. Army.
Enrolled in 13th West Virginia Infantry on August 15, 1862 and mustered
into service on October 9, 1862.
Served as Captain of company C, 13th West Virginia Infantry
U. S. Army records give his age as 26 on October 9, 1862

More About Frances E. Ball:
Burial: Somerville Cemetery, Mason County, West Virginia

　　ii.   William McDaniel, son of Hutchinson McDaniel and Hannah Johnson was born on 25
Sep 1839 in Mason County, Virginia. He died between 04 Jun 1870-06 Jun 1900. He
married Elizabeth Stewart, daughter of William Stewart and Martha Ann Van Sickle
on 19 Dec 1861 in Pleasant Flats, Mason County, Virginia. She was

born on 30 Jan 1839 in Mason County, Virginia. She died on 27 May 1926
in Robinson District, Mason County, West Virginia.

More About William
McDaniel: b: 1839
Occupation: 1870 in Cuivre Township, Pike County, Missouri; Farmer

Notes for William McDaniel:
Probably died in Missouri between June 4, 1870 and December 1, 1879.

More About Elizabeth Stewart:
Burial: 29 May 1926 in Stewart Cemetery, Mason County, West
Virginia Living In: Dec 1879 in Mason County, West Virginia
Living In: 1900 As a widow in Robinson Distict, Mason County, West Virginia.
Living In: 1910 As a widow in Robinson District, Mason County, West Virginia.
Living In: 1920 With her grand daughter, Clara, and her family in Robinson
District, Mason County, West Virginia.
Occupation: 1900 in Robinson District, Mason County, West Virginia; Farmer

Notes for Elizabeth Stewart:
Death certificate gives burial place as Stewart Cemetery. Headstone is present
in Lone Oak Cemetery.

Elizabeth was present at Madaline's wedding to give permission for Madaline to
get married but there is no mention of Madaline's father.
----

9.   iii. Deborah McDaniel, daughter of Hutchinson McDaniel and Hannah Johnson was born on
30 Jul 1843 in Mason County, Virginia. She died on 17 Mar 1900 in Mason County,
West Virginia. She married Henry W. Stewart, son of William Stewart and Martha Ann
Van Sickle on 15 Sep 1862 in Point Pleasant, Mason County, Virginia. He was born on
16 Dec 1830 in Mason County, Virginia. He died on 30 Aug 1905 in West Columbia,
Mason County, West Virginia.

iv.   Mary Ann McDaniel, daughter of Hutchinson McDaniel and Hannah Johnson was
born on 25 Jul 1846 in Mason County, Virginia. She died on 18 Jan 1928 in Pike
County, Missouri. She married John P. Wood, son of George Wood and Mary Ann
(unknown) on 27 Feb 1866 in Point Pleasant, Mason County, West Virginia. He
was born on 12 Feb 1833 in Nelson County, Virginia. He died on 14 Oct 1890 in
Pike County, Missouri.

More About Mary Ann McDaniel:
Burial: Antioch Cemetery, Cyrene, Pike County, Missouri

More About John P. Wood:
Burial: Antioch Cemetery, Cyrene, Pike County, Missouri
Occupation: 1866 in Mason County, West Virginia; Farmer
Occupation: 1870 in Cuivre Township, Pike County, Missouri; Farmer
Occupation: 1880 in Cuivre Township, Pike County, Missouri; Farmer

v. Olevia McDaniel, daughter of Hutchinson McDaniel and Hannah Johnson was born on 15 Dec 1849 in Virginia. She died on 29 Jul 1861 in Virginia.

More About Olevia McDaniel:
Burial: Pioneer Cemetery, Point Pleasant, Mason County, West Virginia

vi. Robert Wesley McDaniel, son of Hutchinson McDaniel and Hannah Johnson was born on 08 Mar 1852 in Virginia. He died on 17 Apr 1924 in Bowie, Montague County, Texas. He married Lucinda P. Burkholder, daughter of Alexander Burkholder and Harriet Penn about 1871. She was born on 08 May 1853 in Virginia. She died on 02 Sep 1940 in Bowie, Montague County, Texas.

More About Robert Wesley McDaniel:
Burial: 18 Apr 1924 in Elmwood Cemetery, Bowie, Montague County,Texas
Cause Of Death: Cancer
Living In: 1880 Precinct 3, Cooke County, Texas
Living In: 1900 Bowie, Montague County, Texas
Occupation: Merchant

More About Lucinda P. Burkholder:
Burial: 03 Sep 1940 in Elmwood Cemetery, Bowie, Montague County,Texas
Living In: 1940 Bowie, Montague County, Texas

vii. John McDaniel, son of Hutchinson McDaniel and Hannah Johnson was born on 11 Aug 1856 in Mason County, Virginia. He died on 11 Aug 1861 in Mason County, Virginia.

More About John McDaniel:
Burial: Pioneer Cemetery, Point Pleasant, Mason County, West Virginia

viii. Patsy J. McDaniel, daughter of Hutchinson McDaniel and Hannah Johnson was born about 1859 in Virginia.

ix. Jessie B. McDaniel, daughter of Hutchinson McDaniel and Hannah Johnson was born about 1863 in Virginia.

20. **George R. Casto**, son of William Casto and Susanna Rollins was born on 26 Jul 1826 in Virginia. He died on 04 Mar 1903 in Parchment Valley, Jackson County, West Virginia. He married **Susanna Dewees**, daughter of Samuel Dewees and Edith Battin on 12 Apr 1845 in Jackson County, Virginia.

21. **Susanna Dewees**, daughter of Samuel Dewees and Edith Battin was born on 20 Oct 1823 in Virginia. She died on 10 Sep 1859 in Jackson County, Virginia.

More About George R. Casto:
Burial: Pleasant Hill Cemetery, Parchment Valley, Jackson County, West Virginia
Cause Of Death: Dropsy
Living In: 1860 George and his children, Samuel, George, Margaret and Edmond are living with his brother William, and his family in Jackson County, Virginia.

Occupation: 1850 in District 27, Jackson County, Virginia; Farmer
Occupation: 1860 in Jackson County, Virginia; Farm Labor
Occupation: 1870 in Union Township, Jackson County, West Virginia; Farmer
Occupation: 1880 in Union District, Jackson County, West Virginia; Laborer
Occupation: 1900 in Ripley District, Jackson County, West Virginia; Farmer

More About Susanna Dewees:
Burial: Pleasant Hill Cemetery, Given, Jackson County, West Virginia
Cause Of Death: Confinement (pregnant)

Notes for Susanna Dewees:
Marriage record has first name as Susan.

Date of death on death record is September 10, 1859. Headstone has April 10, 1857 for date of
death. Death record for John Casto has 1859 for year of death and John being six months old.

More About George R. Casto and Susanna Dewees:
Marriage Fact: Married by E. J. Rollins

Susanna Dewees and George R. Casto had the following children:
    i.   Samuel Daniel Casto, son of George R. Casto and Susanna Dewees was born on
05 Apr 1846 in Jackson County, Virginia. He died on 16 Mar 1923 in Ripley,
Jackson County, West Virginia. He married Mary Emily Flowers, daughter of
Thomas Flowers and Emily Jane Sayre on 29 Dec 1877 in Jackson County, West
Virginia. She was born in Sep 1852 in Virginia. She died before 16 Mar 1923. He
married Amanda Jane Ankrum, daughter of William C. Ankrum and Ruth
(unknown) on 11 Dec 1871 in Jackson County, West Virginia. She was born on 22
Feb 1837 in Jackson County, Virginia. She died on 08 May 1877 in Jackson
County, West Virginia.

More About Samuel Daniel Casto:
Burial: 19 Mar 1923 in United Methodist Church Cemetery, Cottageville,
Jackson County, West Virginia
Cause Of Death: Pneumonia
Living In: 1870 With William C. Ankrum and his family in Jackson County, West
Virginia.
Occupation: Farmer

Notes for Mary Emily Flowers:
Marriage license issued on December 29, 1877.

More About Amanda Jane Ankrum:
Burial: United Methodist Church Cemetery, Cottageville, Jackson County, West
Virginia

Notes for Amanda Jane Ankrum:
Headstone gives her age as 40 years, 2 months and 14 days on May 8, 1877.

10.   ii. George Washington Casto, son of George R. Casto and Susanna Dewees was born on
09 Aug 1847 in Jackson County, Virginia. He died on 13 Nov 1926 in Falls

Township, Hocking County, Ohio. He married Margaret Frances Johnston, daughter of Abraham E. Johnston and Susan L. McMillan on 14 Dec 1878 in Mason County, West Virginia. She was born on 08 Dec 1856 in Grafton, Taylor County, Virginia. She died on 29 Dec 1928 in Marion Township, Franklin County, Ohio. He married Cassandra Catherine Barber, daughter of Sal Barber and C. (unknown) on 20 Sep 1870 in Jackson County, West Virginia. She was born about 1855 in Ohio. She died about 1877.

iii.   Martha Jane Casto, daughter of George R. Casto and Susanna Dewees was born on 16 Dec 1849 in Jackson County, Virginia. She died on 22 Feb 1933 in Millwood, Jackson County, West Virginia. She married Richard Ankrum, son of William C. Ankrum and Ruth (unknown) on 12 Mar 1868 in Jackson County, West Virginia. He was born in Oct 1834 in Tyler County, Virginia. He died on 21 Nov 1909 in Millwood, Jackson County, West Virginia.

More About Martha Jane Casto:
Burial: 24 Feb 1933 in Ankrum Cemetery
Living In: 1860 With Alfred Dewees and his family in Jackson County, Virginia

More About Richard Ankrum:
Cause Of Death: Nephritis

iv.   Lydia Casto, daughter of George R. Casto and Susanna Dewees was born in Jun 1850 in Jackson County, Virginia.

v.   Margaret Casto, daughter of George R. Casto and Susanna Dewees was born about 1853 in Jackson County, Virginia.

vi.   Edmond R. Casto, son of George R. Casto and Susanna Dewees was born in Jan 1857 in Jackson County, Virginia. He died in Mar 1877 in Mason County, West Virginia.

vii.   John Casto, son of George R. Casto and Susanna Dewees was born in 1859 in Jackson County, Virginia. He died in 1859 in Jackson County, Virginia.

More About John Casto:
Cause Of Death: Bowel Complications

Notes for John Casto:
Lived for six months.

22.   **Abraham E. Johnston** was born on 30 Jan 1828 in Taylor County, Virginia. He died on 06 Oct 1886 in Jackson County, West Virginia. He married **Susan L. McMillan**.

23.   **Susan L. McMillan** was born in Sep 1834 in Virginia. She died after 26 Jun 1900.

More About Abraham E. Johnston:
Occupation: 1850 in District 38, Mason County, Virginia; Farmer
Occupation: 1854 in Monongalia County, Virginia; Farmer
Occupation: 1860 in Taylor County, Virginia; Farm Labor
Occupation: 1880 in Cologne District, Mason County, West Virginia; Farm Laborer

More About Susan L. McMillan:
Living In: 1900 With her son, John, in Cologne District, Mason County, West Virginia

Notes for Susan L. McMillan:
James McMillan, Shoe Maker, born about 1785 in Virginia, is living with Abraham and Susan in 1850. Possibly Susan's father.

Susan L. McMillan and Abraham E. Johnston had the following children:

i.   Nancy Isabel Johnston, daughter of Abraham E. Johnston and Susan L. McMillan was born on 26 Dec 1849 in Mason County, Virginia. She died on 30 Jun 1865 in Taylor County, West Virginia.

ii.   John N. Johnston, son of Abraham E. Johnston and Susan L. McMillan was born in May 1852 in Ohio.

More About John N. Johnston:
Living In: 1880 With his parents in Cologne District, Mason County, West Virginia.

iii.   James A. Johnston, son of Abraham E. Johnston and Susan L. McMillan was born on 14 Sep 1854 in Paulding County, Ohio.

More About James A. Johnston:
Living In: 1880 With his parents in Cologne District, Mason County, West Virginia.

11.   iv. Margaret Frances Johnston, daughter of Abraham E. Johnston and Susan L. McMillan was born on 08 Dec 1856 in Grafton, Taylor County, Virginia. She died on 29 Dec 1928 in Marion Township, Franklin County, Ohio. She married George Washington Casto, son of George R. Casto and Susanna Dewees on 14 Dec 1878 in Mason County, West Virginia. He was born on 09 Aug 1847 in Jackson County, Virginia. He died on 13 Nov 1926 in Falls Township, Hocking County, Ohio.

vi.   Arvilla Johnston, son of Abraham E. Johnston and Susan L. McMillan was born on 20 Feb 1859 in Taylor County, West Virginia.

vi.   Mary Johnston, daughter of Abraham E. Johnston and Susan L. McMillan was born about 1862 in Virginia.

vii.   Hesekiah Elsworth Johnston, son of Abraham E. Johnston and Susan L. McMillan was born about 1865 in Taylor county, West Virginia. He married Annie Gerutha Seters on 03 May 1884 in Mason County, West Virginia. She was born about 1868 in Meigs County, Ohio.

More About Hesekiah Elsworth Johnston and Annie Gerutha Seters: Marriage Fact: Married in the residence of the bride.

viii.   Hellen Johnston, daughter of Abraham E. Johnston and Susan L. McMillan was born about 1867 in West Virginia.

ix.   Franklin Johnston, son of Abraham E. Johnston and Susan L. McMillan was born about 1871 in West Virginia.

x. William Johnston, son of Abraham E. Johnston and Susan L. McMillan was born about 1873 in West Virginia.

xi. Clarabell Johnston, daughter of Abraham E. Johnston and Susan L. McMillan was born about 1877 in West Virginia.

24. **Wesley Summers Tucker**, son of Henry William Tucker and Anna Roby was born on 03 Apr 1834 in Leesburg, Carroll County, Ohio. He died on 14 Aug 1906 in Goodhope Township, Hocking County, Ohio. He married **Phebe Hutson**, daughter of James Hutson and Ellenor Clark on 01 May 1856 in Hocking County, Ohio.

25. **Phebe Hutson**, daughter of James Hutson and Ellenor Clark was born on 18 May 1834 in Carroll County, Ohio. She died on 18 Nov 1905 in Lancaster, Ohio.

More About Wesley Summers Tucker:
Burial: Fairview Methodist Church Cemetery, Good Hope Township, Hocking County, Ohio
Living In: 1850 With his half sister, Etheldra, and her family in Dover Township, Tuscarawas County, Ohio.
Living In: 1890 Goodhope Township, Hocking County, Ohio
Occupation: 1850 in Dover Township, Tuscarawas County, Ohio; Chair Maker
Occupation: 1860 in New Lexington, Perry County, Ohio; Carpenter
Occupation: 1870 in Laurel Township, Hocking County, Ohio; Cabinet Maker
Occupation: 1880 in Laurel Township, Hocking County, Ohio; Working on Saw Mill
Occupation: 1900 in Rockbridge, Good Hope Township, Hocking County, Ohio; Proprietor of Planning Mill
Military Service: Bet. 04 Aug 1861-16 Aug 1863; Company B, 31st Ohio Infantry, U.S. Army
Property: 1870 in Laurel Township, Hocking County, Ohio; 25 acres Improved and 18 Acres Unimproved

Notes for Wesley Summers Tucker:
Mustered out of the U.S. Army at Camp Thomas, near Columbus, Ohio.

Registered for draft June 1863 in Laurel Township, Hocking County, Ohio.

More About Phebe Hutson:
Burial: Fairview Methodist Church Cemetery, Good Hope Township, Hocking County, Ohio

Notes for Phebe Hutson:
Ohio death index gives birth year as 1834. 1900 U.S. census gives birth date as May 1834. Headstone gives birth year as 1834.

First name is from her headstone.

Phebe Hutson and Wesley Summers Tucker had the following children:
i. Joseph B. Tucker, son of Wesley Summers Tucker and Phebe Hutson was born on 02 Feb 1857 in Hocking County, Ohio. He died on 13 Jun 1926 in Columbus, Franklin County, Ohio. He married Nellie May Blackburn, daughter of William Blackburn and Hannah McGraco on 23 Dec 1880 in Hocking County, Ohio. She was born on 15 Aug 1858 in Pickaway County, Ohio. She died on 06 Nov 1935 in Columbus, Franklin County, Ohio.

More About Joseph B. Tucker:
Burial: 15 Jun 1926 in Greenlawn Cemetery, Columbus, Franklin County, Ohio
Living In: 1880 With his parents in Laurel Township, Hocking County, Ohio.
Occupation: 1870 in Laurel Township, Hocking County, Ohio; Farm Worker
Occupation: 1880 in Laurel Township, Hocking County, Ohio; Farmer
Occupation: 1900 in Lancaster, Fairfield County, Ohio; Common Labor
Occupation: 1910 in Lancaster, Fairfield County, Ohio; General Work Laborer
Occupation: 1920 in Columbus, Franklin County, Ohio; Railroad Shop Labor

More About Nellie May Blackburn:
Burial: 09 Nov 1935 in Greenlawn Cemetery, Columbus, Franklin County, Ohio
Living In: 1930 With her son, Arthur, and his family in Columbus, Franklin County, Ohio.

Notes for Nellie May Blackburn:
Ohio Marriage Records have name listed as Ellie Blackburn.

12.   ii. Hollis Clark Tucker, son of Wesley Summers Tucker and Phebe Hutson was born on 15 Aug 1858 in Hocking County, Ohio. He died on 25 Apr 1916 in Columbus, Franklin County, Ohio. He married Clara Fox, daughter of Peter Fox and Deborah White on 16 Feb 1879 in Hocking County, Ohio. She was born on 27 Sep 1857 in Laurel Township, Hocking County, Ohio. She died on 30 Dec 1923 in Laurelville, Hocking County, Ohio. He married Eliza Lucretia Huls, daughter of David William Huls and Eliza Ann Peters on 12 Jul 1893 in Hocking County, Ohio. She was born on 19 Jan 1875 in Hocking County, Ohio. She died on 21 Nov 1960 in Hocking County, Ohio.

iii.   Sarah Sarvilla Tucker, daughter of Wesley Summers Tucker and Phebe Hutson was born on 20 May 1860 in New Lexington, Perry County, Ohio. She died on 04 Jun 1871 in Laurel Township, Hocking County, Ohio.

iv.   Betty Emma Tucker, daughter of Wesley Summers Tucker and Phebe Hutson was born on 17 Feb 1862 in Ohio. She died on 01 Oct 1863 in Ohio.

v.   Ella Somorrah Tucker, daughter of Wesley Summers Tucker and Phebe Hutson was born on 09 Mar 1866 in Ohio. She died on 21 Aug 1885 in Tennessee.

More About Ella Somorrah Tucker:
Burial: Mount Ararat Cemetery, Lawrence County, Tennessee

vi.   James Henry Tucker, son of Wesley Summers Tucker and Phebe Hutson was born on 25 Apr 1873 in Laurel Township, Hocking County, Ohio. He died on 27 Feb 1878 in Laurel Township, Hocking County, Ohio.

26.   **Peter Fox**, son of John Fox and Nancy Julien was born on 06 Jan 1814 in Laurel Township, Hocking County, Ohio. He died on 08 Feb 1890 in Hocking County, Ohio. He married **Deborah White**, daughter of James White on 04 Mar 1838 in Perry County, Ohio.

27.   **Deborah White**, daughter of James White was born on 14 Feb 1817 in Hocking County, Ohio. She died on 16 Jan 1900 in Hocking County, Ohio.

More About Peter Fox:

Burial: Mount Olive Cemetery, South Perry, Hocking County, Ohio
Occupation: Bet. 1840-1880 in Laurel Township, Hocking County, Ohio; Farmer
Property: 1870 in Laurel Township, Hocking County, Ohio; 70 Acres Improved and 40
Acres Unimproved

More About Deborah White:
Burial: Mount Olive Cemetery, South Perry, Hocking County, Ohio

Deborah White and Peter Fox had the following children:

    i.   Nancy Fox, daughter of Peter Fox and Deborah White was born on 07 Jan 1839 in Ohio. She died on 07 Jul 1925 in Laurelville, Hocking County, Ohio. She married Jacob B. Riason, son of Reason Riason and Annie Brown on 06 Jan 1860 in Hocking County, Ohio. He was born on 17 Apr 1838 in Ohio. He died on 25 May 1916 in Laurelville, Hocking, Ohio, USA.

    More About Nancy Fox:
    Burial: 09 Jul 1925 in Green Summit Cemetery, Adelphi, Ross County, Ohio

    More About Jacob B. Riason:
    Burial: 27 May 1916 in Green Summit Cemetery, Adelphi, Ross County, Ohio
    Occupation: Lawyer

    ii.   Jacob Fox, son of Peter Fox and Deborah White was born about 1841 in Ohio.

    iii.   Mary Fox, daughter of Peter Fox and Deborah White was born on 07 Nov 1842 in Laurel Township, Hocking County, Ohio. She died on 07 Sep 1932 in Perry Township, Hocking County, Ohio. She married Alfred Stump, son of Samuel E. Stump and Mary Cave on 01 Mar 1868 in Hocking County, Ohio. He was born on 04 Nov 1845 in Ohio. He died on 24 Oct 1930 in Perry Township, Hocking County, Ohio.

    More About Mary Fox:
    Burial: 09 Sep 1932 in Morgan Chapel Cemetery, Hocking County, Ohio

    More About Alfred Stump:
    Burial: 26 Oct 1930 in Morgan Chapel Cemetery, Hocking County, Ohio
    Cause Of Death: Accidental burns when clothing caught on fire October 19, 1930.

    iv.   Martha Fox, daughter of Peter Fox and Deborah White was born about 1845 in Ohio.

    v.   Matilda Fox, daughter of Peter Fox and Deborah White was born on 30 Mar 1847 in Ohio. She died on 30 Jan 1929 in Salt Creek Township, Pickaway County, Ohio. She married Simon Judy, son of Simon Judy and Ann Shearer on 07 Sep 1865 in Hocking County, Ohio. He was born on 12 Feb 1841 in Fairfield County, (now Hocking County), Ohio. He died on 07 Apr 1931 in Clearcreek Township, Fairfield County, Ohio.

More About Matilda Fox:
Burial: 01 Feb 1929 in Tarlton Cemetery, Tarlton, Pickaway County, Ohio
Living In: 1929 Laurelville, Hocking County, Ohio

More About Simon Judy:
Burial: 09 Apr 1931 in Tarlton Cemetery, Tarlton, Pickaway County, Ohio

vi.   Elizabeth Fox, daughter of Peter Fox and Deborah White was born about 1849 in Ohio. She died between 08 Jun 1880-23 Mar 1885 in Ohio. She married Nelson Hedges, son of Charles Hedges and Sarah (unknown) on 03 Oct 1867 in Hocking County, Ohio. He was born on 06 Jul 1846 in Ohio. He died on 12 Dec 1916 in Perry Township, Hocking County, Ohio.

More About Nelson Hedges:
Burial: 14 Dec 1916 in Pleasant Ridge Cemetery, Laurelville, Hocking County, Ohio
Cause Of Death: Gunshot wound and resulting shock.

vii.   Sarah Fox, daughter of Peter Fox and Deborah White was born on 08 Jul 1853 in Hocking County, Ohio. She died on 11 Nov 1926 in Delaware, Delaware County, Ohio. She married Stephan Rizer, son of Henry Rizer and Martha Mauler on 13 May 1869 in Hocking County, Ohio. He was born on 13 Jul 1848 in Athens County, Ohio. He died on 03 Mar 1924 in Westerville, Franklin County, Ohio.

More About Sarah Fox:
Burial: 14 Nov 1926 in Westerville, Ohio
Living In: 1926 Columbus, Franklin County, Ohio

viii.   Ellen Fox, daughter of Peter Fox and Deborah White was born on 30 Mar 1855 in Ohio. She died on 29 Mar 1918 in Salt Creek Township, Pickaway County, Ohio. She married Daniel Fetherolf, son of Daniel Fetherolf and Rebecca (unknown) on 01 Dec 1875 in Hocking County, Ohio. He was born on 20 Oct 1850 in Hocking County, Ohio. He died on 29 Mar 1947 in Circleville, Pickaway County, Ohio.

More About Ellen Fox:
Burial: 01 Apr 1918 in Prarieview Cemetery, Whisler, Pickaway County, Ohio

More About Daniel Fetherolf:
Burial: 31 Mar 1947 in Prarieview Cemetery, Whisler, Pickaway County, Ohio

13.   ix. Clara Fox, daughter of Peter Fox and Deborah White was born on 27 Sep 1857 in Laurel Township, Hocking County, Ohio. She died on 30 Dec 1923 in Laurelville, Hocking County, Ohio. She married Hollis Clark Tucker, son of Wesley Summers Tucker and Phebe Hutson on 16 Feb 1879 in Hocking County, Ohio. He was born on 15 Aug 1858 in Hocking County, Ohio. He died on 25 Apr 1916 in Columbus, Franklin County, Ohio. She married William Cook, son of John Cook and Nancy Price about 1875. He was born on 16 Sep 1857 in Green Township, Hocking County, Ohio. He died on 25 Apr 1919 in West Salem Township, Mercer County,

Pennsylvania. She married Aaron Stahr on 16 Mar 1893 in Hocking County, Ohio. He was born on 21 Jun 1867 in Germany. He died on 14 May 1950 in Eaton, Preble County, Ohio.

28.   **Levi Davis**, son of John W. Davis and (Unknown) was born on 01 Jul 1805 in Loudoun County, Virginia. He died on 06 Jun 1885 in Falls Township, Hocking County, Ohio. He married **Mary Ann Rodman** on 15 Aug 1830 in Muskingum County, ohio.

29.   **Mary Ann Rodman** was born about 1812 in Pennsylvania. She died on 01 Dec 1886 in Falls Township, Hocking County, Ohio.

More About Levi Davis:
Occupation: 1850 in Falls Township, Hocking County, Ohio; Surveyor and Farmer
Occupation: 1860 in Falls Township, Hocking County, Ohio; Surveyor
Occupation: 1870 in Falls Township, Hocking County, Ohio; Surveyor
Occupation: 1880 in Falls Township, Hocking County, Ohio; Engineer

Notes for Levi Davis:
        (from chapter 36, 1883 History of Hocking Valley)
Levi Davis, civil engineer and surveyor, of Hocking County,
was born in Loudoun County, Va., near Leesburg, July 1, 1805, a
son of John W. and Elizabeth (Hesser) Davis. When he was nine
years of age his parents moved to Fairfax County, Va., remaining
there four years, when they removed to Prince William County,
and three years later returned to Loudoun County. In 1823 they
came to Ohio, first settling near Hanover, Columbiana County. Mr.
Davis received his rudimentary education in the common schools,
but by private personal application acquired a mathematical and
scientific education, and after years of careful study, obtained a
practical knowledge of civil engineering and surveying, being one
of the best of that profession in the State. When twenty years of
age he left home and was employed as a laborer on the public
works of the Ohio Canal six months, when he was appointed
superintendent of the canal construction, retaining that position
till 1830. The next three years he was a contractor on the National
turnpike road in Muskingum County, and in 1833 was appointed by
the Government as superintendent of construction for a section of
fifteen miles of the same turnpike in Licking and Franklin counties. In
1836 he resigned his position and was a contractor on the Sandy
and Beaver Canal in Columbiana County till 1838, when he was
employed as superintendent of construction on the slack water
works of Muskingum River till 1839. From that year till 1842 he
taught school in Muskingum County, when he came to Hocking
County and settled two miles south of Logan, where he still resides.
In 1844 he was elected County Surveyor of Hocking County, holding
the position thirty years, when, in 1874, on ac-count of his age, he
declined re-election, and his son, James W., was elected in his
stead. Aug. 15, 1830, Mr. Davis married Mary Ann Rodman, of
Muskingum County. They have had a family of thirteen children,
eight of whom are still living---John R., born Aug. 15, 1831; Sarah J.,
Oct. 5, 1833, now Mrs. John Shields; Samuel G., born March 12,
1835, died Nov. 9, 1836; Wesley A., born July 18, 1837; Levi, May
11, 1839, married Mary Bigham; Mary R., born May 5, 1841, died
May 13, 1841; Lycurgus, born April 3, 1842; James W., July 4,
1844; Eliza A., Nov. 20, 1846; Samantha (Mrs. Jones), May 7, 1849,
died in 1880; Edith C., born April 3, 1852, died April 7, 1854; Harriet
M., born Feb. 18, 1855;

Lucellus, Oct. 30, 1859, died Sept. 22, 1863.

Age at death on death record would give birth date of June 12, 1805.

Notes for Mary Ann Rodman:
A second death record gives her date of death as November 30, 1886 in Laurel Township, Hocking County, Ohio, married and born about 1812 in Pennsylvania.

The December 1, 1886 Falls Township, Hocking County, Ohio death record lists her as widowed and born about 1812 in Pennsylvania.

Mary Ann Rodman and Levi Davis had the following children:

    i.   John R. Davis, son of Levi Davis and Mary Ann Rodman was born on 15 Aug 1831 in Ohio.

    ii.   Sarah Jane Davis, daughter of Levi Davis and Mary Ann Rodman was born on 05 Oct 1833 in Ohio. She died after 13 Jun 1900. She married John Shields before 15 Jun 1880. He was born about 1831 in Ohio. He died on 22 Jun 1886 in Ward Township, Hocking County, Ohio. She married Eli Westenhaver on 03 Aug 1848 in Hocking County, Ohio. He was born about 1825 in Ohio. She married George B. Otis on 17 Dec 1855 in Hocking County, Ohio. He was born about 1835 in New York.

More About Sarah Jane Davis:
Living In: 1900 With her step son, Curtis Shields, in Carbon Hill Precinct, Ward Township, Hocking County, Ohio.

More About John Shields:
Occupation: 1880 in Ward Township, Hocking County, Ohio; Butcher

More About Eli Westenhaver:
Living In: 1850 Green Township, Hocking County, Ohio

More About George B. Otis:
Occupation: 1860 in York Township, Athens County, Ohio; Coal Rigger
Occupation: 1880 in Ward Township, Hocking County, Ohio; Coal Miner

    iii.   Samuel G. Davis, son of Levi Davis and Mary Ann Rodman was born on 12 Mar 1835 in Ohio. He died on 09 Nov 1836 in Ohio.

    iv.   Wesley A. Davis, son of Levi Davis and Mary Ann Rodman was born on 18 Jul 1837 in Ohio. He married Nancy Barstow on 12 Sep 1861 in Hocking County, Ohio. She was born about 1838 in Ohio.

More About Wesley A. Davis:
Living In: 1870 With his parents in Falls Township, Hocking County, Ohio.
Occupation: 1870 in Green Township, Hocking County, Ohio; Farmer

14.   v. Levi Davis, son of Levi Davis and Mary Ann Rodman was born on 11 May 1839 in Muskingum County, ohio. He died on 08 Apr 1909 in Perry Township, Hocking

County, Ohio. He married Mary Ann Bigham, daughter of Isaac Bigham and Mary Elizabeth Delong on 10 Mar 1875 in Hocking County, Ohio. She was born on 15 Feb 1855 in Hocking County, Ohio. She died on 07 Aug 1924 in Greenfield Township, Fairfield County, Ohio. He married Mary B. Shultz, daughter of David Shultz and Mary J. Biers on 13 Oct 1859 in Hocking County, Ohio. She was born in 1839 in Ohio. She died on 05 May 1874 in Muskingum County, Ohio.

vi.   Mary R. Davis, daughter of Levi Davis and Mary Ann Rodman was born on 05 May 1841 in Ohio. She died on 13 May 1841 in Ohio.

vii. Lycurgus Davis, son of Levi Davis and Mary Ann Rodman was born on 03 Apr 1842 in Ohio. He died on 07 May 1895 in Zanesville, Muskingum County, Ohio. He married Emaline Bartholow on 16 Aug 1866 in Hocking County, Ohio. She was born about 1851 in Ohio. He married Mattie Johnson on 12 Jun 1887 in Muskingum County, Ohio. She was born in Oct 1848 in Ohio.

More About Lycurgus Davis:
Burial: Greenwood Cemetery, Zanesville, Muskingum County, Ohio
Occupation: 1870 in Hopewell Township, Muskingum County, Ohio; Laborer
Occupation: 1880 in Falls Township, Hocking County, Ohio; Laborer
Military Service: Bet. 21 Oct 1861-08 Jul 1865; Company H, 63rd Ohio Infantry, U. S. Army

Notes for Lycurgus Davis:
Only his daughter, Bella, is living with him in 1880. His son, Charles, is boarding with Savina Shultz. His wife is not mentioned in the 1880 census report.

Mustered out of Company H, 63rd Ohio Infantry on July 8, 1865 at Louisville, Kentucky.

More About Mattie Johnson:
Living In: 1900 Zanesville, Muskingum County, Ohio
Living In: 1920 With her niece, Minnie Craig, in Zanesville, Muskingum County, Ohio.

viii. James William Davis, son of Levi Davis and Mary Ann Rodman was born on 04 Jul 1844 in Logan, Falls Township, Hocking County, Ohio. He died on 13 Nov 1904 in Logan, Hocking County, Ohio. He married Almeda A. Main, daughter of William Main and Belinda Green on 11 Sep 1866 in Hocking County, Ohio. She was born on 29 Apr 1849 in Logan, Falls Township, Hocking County, Ohio. She died on 30 Jan 1928 in Logan, Hocking County, Ohio.

More About James William Davis:
Burial: Shaw Cemetery, Hocking County, Ohio
Occupation: 1870 in Falls Township, Hocking County, Ohio; Farm Laborer
Occupation: 1880 in Falls Township, Hocking County, Ohio; Surveyor
Occupation: 1900 in Falls Township, Hocking County, Ohio; Civil Engineer
Military Service: Bet. Jul 1861-Jul 1865 in Company B, 31st Ohio Infantry, U.S. Army

Notes for James William Davis:

(from 1883 History of Hocking County)
James William Davis, County Surveyor of Hocking County, was born in Falls Township, near Logan, July 4, 1844, a son of Levi and Mary A. (Rodman) Davis. In July, 1861, he enlisted in Company B, Thirty-first Ohio Infantry, to serve three years. In January, 1864, he veteranized and served till the close of the war, serving as Corporal from his last enlistment. He was in the battles of Mill Springs, Shiloh, Hoover's Gap, Chickamauga, Stone River, Chattanooga, and in the campaign to Atlanta, and from there with Sherman to the sea. He was discharged in July, 1865, at Camp Chase, Ohio. After a short visit at home he went to Louisville, Ky., and remained two years, when he returned to Logan. His father being a civil engineer he also studied the science, and in 1872 was elected his father's successor as County Surveyor, and has since filled that position, he having filled the same position over thirty years. Sept. 11, 1866, Mr. Davis married Almeda Mane, of Falls Township. They have two children---Ada and Otto.

More About Almeda A. Main:
Burial: 02 Feb 1928 in Shaw Cemetery, Hocking County, Ohio
Living In: 1910 Logan, Hocking County, Ohio
Living In: 1920 Logan, Hocking County, Ohio

Notes for Almeda A. Main:
Name on her marriage record is spelled "Almeda Main". Father's name on her death certificate is spelled "William Main".

----

ix. Eliza A. Davis, daughter of Levi Davis and Mary Ann Rodman was born on 20 Nov 1846 in Logan, Hocking county, OhioOhio. She married John W. Sniff, son of Isaiah Sniff and Elizabeth Moore on 25 Dec 1866 in Hocking County, Ohio. He was born on 13 Feb 1842 in Vinton County, Ohio. He died on 16 Jan 1904 in Falls Township, Hocking County, Ohio. She married Charles Simpson, son of Charles Simpson and Jemima Sutton on 10 Apr 1908 in Hocking County, Ohio. He was born on 31 Mar 1853 in Pittsburgh, Allegheny County, Pennsylvania.

More About John W. Sniff:
Living In: 1870 Starr Township, Hocking County, Ohio
Living In: 1880 Falls Township, Hocking County, Ohio
Living In: 1900 Falls Township, Hocking County, Ohio
Occupation: Farmer

Notes for John W. Sniff:
Birth date is from age at death on death record.

x. Samantha Davis, daughter of Levi Davis and Mary Ann Rodman was born on 07 May 1849 in Ohio. She died in 1880. She married (unknown) Jones.

xi. Edith C. Davis, daughter of Levi Davis and Mary Ann Rodman was born on 03 Apr 1852 in Ohio. She died on 07 Apr 1854 in Ohio.

xii. Harriet M. Davis, daughter of Levi Davis and Mary Ann Rodman was born on 18 Feb 1855 in Ohio. She died on 16 Nov 1880.

xiii. Lucellus Davis, son of Levi Davis and Mary Ann Rodman was born on 30 Oct 1859 in Ohio. He died on 22 Sep 1863.

30. **Isaac Bigham**, son of Samuel Bigham and Sarah Morris was born on 10 Mar 1828 in Guernsey County, Ohio. He died on 29 Nov 1896 in Laurel Township, Hocking County, Ohio. He married **Mary Elizabeth Delong**, daughter of Samuel Franklin Delong and Mary Ann Kimble on 16 Apr 1850 in Hocking County, Ohio.

31. **Mary Elizabeth Delong**, daughter of Samuel Franklin Delong and Mary Ann Kimble was born on 19 Jan 1831 in Laurel Township, Hocking County, Ohio. She died on 30 Jun 1877 in Hocking County, Ohio.

More About Isaac Bigham:
Burial: Brown Cemetery, Good Hope Township, Hocking County, Ohio
Occupation: 1850 in Good Hope Township, Hocking County, Ohio; Farmer
Occupation: 1860 in Laurel Township, Hocking County, Ohio; Farmer
Occupation: 1870 in Laurel Township, Hocking County, Ohio; Farmer
Occupation: 1880 in Laurel Township, Hocking County, Ohio; Farmer

More About Mary Elizabeth Delong:
Burial: Betheny Church Cemetery, Hocking County, Ohio

Mary Elizabeth Delong and Isaac Bigham had the following children:
i. Abraham Bigham, son of Isaac Bigham and Mary Elizabeth Delong was born on 03 Jul 1849 in Hocking County, Ohio. He died on 02 May 1931 in Perry Township, Hocking County, Ohio. He married Margaret Byers, daughter of John S. Byers and Nancy Eaton on 13 Oct 1870 in Hocking County, Ohio. He married Seenith Croy on 22 Sep 1877 in Hocking County, Ohio. She was born in May 1853 in Ohio. He married Matilda McGrady, daughter of Unknown and Ellen McGrady on 15 Apr 1914. She was born on 29 Jan 1869 in Hocking County, Ohio. She died on 25 Nov 1941 in Perry Township, Hocking County, Ohio.

More About Abraham Bigham:
Burial: 04 May 1931 in Pisgah Church Cemetery, Hocking County, Ohio
Cause Of Death: Cardiac Insufficiency
Occupation: Farmer

More About Matilda McGrady:
Burial: 28 Nov 1941 in Pisgah Cemetery, Good Hope Township, Hocking County, Ohio

ii. Samuel Bigham, son of Isaac Bigham and Mary Elizabeth Delong was born on 11 Oct 1851 in Hocking County, Ohio. He died on 16 Jan 1922 in Lancaster, Fairfield County, Ohio. He married Charlotte E. Teeter, daughter of Curtis W. Teeter and Mary Essford on 16 Sep 1871 in Hocking County, Ohio. She was born on 27 Oct 1848 in Newark, Licking County, Ohio. She died on 24 Apr 1910 in Lancaster,

Fairfield County, Ohio.

More About Samuel Bigham:
Burial: 19 Jan 1922 in Brown Cemetery, Goodhope Township, Hocking County, Ohio
Cause Of Death: Chronic Myocarditis
Occupation: Farmer

More About Charlotte E. Teeter:
Burial: 26 Apr 1910 in Brown Cemetery, Goodhope Township, Hocking County, Ohio

iii. William Bigham, son of Isaac Bigham and Mary Elizabeth Delong was born on 09 Jan 1852 in Hocking County, Ohio. He died on 15 Jun 1918 in Pleasant Township, Fairfield County, Ohio. He married Rebecca Ann Croy, daughter of Samuel Croy and Eliza Bobo on 25 Oct 1875 in Hocking County, Ohio. She was born on 06 Apr 1854 in Athens, Ohio. She died on 06 May 1945 in Logan, Ohio.

More About William Bigham:
Burial: 17 Jun 1918 in Betheny Church Cemetery, Hocking County, Ohio Cause Of Death: Aortic Stenosis
Occupation: Farmer

15. iv. Mary Ann Bigham, daughter of Isaac Bigham and Mary Elizabeth Delong was born on 15 Feb 1855 in Hocking County, Ohio. She died on 07 Aug 1924 in Greenfield Township, Fairfield County, Ohio. She married Levi Davis, son of Levi Davis and Mary Ann Rodman on 10 Mar 1875 in Hocking County, Ohio. He was born on 11 May 1839 in Muskingum County, ohio. He died on 08 Apr 1909 in Perry Township, Hocking County, Ohio. She married Nathaniel P. Springer, son of John Springer between 08 Apr 1909-04 May 1910. He was born on 24 May 1827 in Perry County, Ohio. He died on 28 Oct 1922 in Perry Township, Hocking County, Ohio. She married William Walton, son of Boaz Walton and Margaret Burress on 27 Sep 1923 in Franklin County, Ohio. He was born on 17 Aug 1844 in New Philadelphia, Tuscarawas County, Ohio. He died on 19 Feb 1930 in Benton Township, Hocking County, Ohio.

v. Sarah Bigham, daughter of Isaac Bigham and Mary Elizabeth Delong was born on 18 Oct 1856 in Hocking County, Ohio. She died on 30 Apr 1926 in Washington Township, Hocking County, Ohio. She married Daniel Nixon on 27 Oct 1887 in Hocking County, Ohio. He was born on 13 Nov 1825 in Ohio. He died on 09 Nov 1907 in Athens County, Ohio. She married James Fox, son of James Fox and Nancy Clutter on 23 Jan 1873 in Hocking County, Ohio. He was born on 11 Oct 1851 in Hocking County, Ohio. He died on 14 Jul 1884 in Laurel Township, Hocking County, Ohio.

More About Sarah Bigham:
Burial: 03 May 1926 in Ewing Cemetery, Ewing, Hocking County, Ohio

More About Daniel Nixon:
Burial: Scott Creek Cemetery, Hocking County, Ohio

More About James Fox:

Burial: Brown Cemetery, Good Hope Township, Hocking County,
Ohio Cause Of Death: Consumption

Notes for James Fox:
Birth date is from age at death on head stone.

----

vi.   Eliza Bigham, daughter of Isaac Bigham and Mary Elizabeth Delong was
       born about 1858 in Hocking County, Ohio. She died after 01 Jun 1870.

       Notes   for   Eliza
       Bigham: Died young.

vii.   Byron Bigham, son of Isaac Bigham and Mary Elizabeth Delong was born
       about Mar 1860 in Hocking County, Ohio. He died before 01 Jun 1870.

viii. Isaac Wesley Bigham, son of Isaac Bigham and Mary Elizabeth Delong was
       born on 26 Apr 1861 in Hocking County, Ohio. He died on 01 Feb 1923 in Perry
       Township, Hocking County, Ohio. He married Zelda Clapper, daughter of Jacob
       Clapper and Savilla Bowman on 11 Aug 1881 in Hocking County, Ohio. She
       was born on 05 Feb 1858 in Hocking County, Ohio. She died on 03 Nov 1922 in
       Perry Township, Hocking County, Ohio.

       More About Isaac Wesley Bigham:
       Burial: 04 Feb 1923 in Pisgah Church Cemetery, Hocking County,
       Ohio
       Cause Of Death: Organic Heart Trouble
       Occupation: Farmer

       More About Zelda Clapper:
       Burial: 05 Nov 1922 in Pisgah Cemetery, Good Hope Township, Hocking
       County, Ohio

       Notes for Zelda Clapper:
       Headstone has February 5, 1858 for date of birth. Death certificate has
       December 25, 1857 for date of birth.

       ----

ix.   Jacob Bigham, son of Isaac Bigham and Mary Elizabeth Delong was born on 03
       Nov 1862 in Hocking County, Ohio. He died on 20 Aug 1928 in Laurel, Hocking
       County, Ohio. He married Rachel Deborah Seesholtz, daughter of Henry G.
       Seesholtz and Catherine Ebert on 14 Feb 1883 in Hocking County, Ohio. She
       was born on 11 Nov 1863 in South Perry, Hocking County, Ohio. She died on 24
       Oct 1951 in Sugar Grove, Fairfield County, Ohio.

       More About Jacob Bigham:
       Burial: 22 Aug 1928 in Forest Rose Cemetery, Lancaster, Fairfield County,
       Ohio
       Cause Of Death: Septicemia
       Occupation: Farmer

More About Rachel Deborah Seesholtz:
Burial: 27 Oct 1951 in Forest Rose Cemetery, Lancaster, Fairfield County, Ohio

x.   Joseph Bigham, son of Isaac Bigham and Mary Elizabeth Delong was born on
     11 May 1863 in Hocking County, Ohio. He died on 24 Jul 1895 in Perry
     Township, Hocking County, Ohio. He married Louisa Anna Hendrickson,
     daughter of George Hendrickson and Mary Leisure on 03 Apr 1886 in Hocking
     County, Ohio. She was born on 12 Apr 1867 in Hocking County, Ohio. She died
     on 14 Jan 1899 in Perry Township, Hocking County, Ohio.

     More About Joseph Bigham:
     Burial: Pisgah Church Cemetery, Good Hope Township, Hocking County, Ohio

     Notes for Joseph Bigham:
     Headstone has 1896 for year of
     death.

     Bigham and Benway
      by Konrad Stump, contributing writer to The Logan Daily News.

     In each of our family histories, there are stories we have heard that stick with us,
     a lot of the time because they involve something that isn't quite explained or
     understood. Sometimes they are mentioned in passing, and sometimes the
     stories are known but there are elements that have been told incorrectly. The
     descendants of Joseph Bigham and Oliver Benway may know something of the
     story of their deaths, but we'd all like an account of the stories that have been
     passed down in pieces.

     It was Wednesday, July 24, 1895. It was about 9 a.m. At his home in the
     northwestern part of Laurel Township, near Cantwell Cliffs, Joseph Bigham had
     been digging a well. He was preparing to build a new house, having made the
     excavation for the cellar and starting work on this well. He was being assisted but
     his brother-in-law, Oliver Benway. The evening before, they fired a blast in the well
     in order to get fire to burn in it, but it didn't do any good. They left the house about
     seven o'clock on Wednesday morning to work on the well. Joseph went down in
     the well, but was overcome by carbonic acid gas, which at the time was commonly
     called well damp. He called to Oliver to pull him up, but was too affected by the
     gas to hold the rope. Oliver called out for help. Mary Yantes, who was staying with
     the Bighams at the time, and Joseph's wife Anna, came to assist. Oliver lowered
     himself into the well, fanning Joseph for a few minutes in an attempt to revive him,
     but soon felt himself being overcome by the gas. He called for the women to pull
     him up; they were able to get him up about 16 to 17 feet, but he was so overcome
     by the gas he fell back to the bottom of the well, which at the time was about 35
     feet deep.

     Mary ran to the nearest neighbors about a half-mile away, and a group of men came
     back with her to assist. Dan Kline went down in the well to retrieve the men, but only
     got about half way before the gas overcame him and he needed to be pulled out.
     They pumped air into the well by means of a windmill and sheet, and a burning sheaf
     of wheat was lowered into it. Dan went back down in the bucket, tied a rope around
     the bodies of Joseph and Oliver, and brought them up. They had been dead for some
     time, it having been over an hour since Oliver first called for help. Oliver's head was
     badly cut from when he'd fallen back into the well.

The funerals took place at Mt. Pisgah, with the Rev. Mather officiating. Mather's sermon was delivered outside, as the people who'd come to attend the funerals couldn't fit in the church. People who were there guessed the attendees numbered around one thousand.

Here is what I can tell you of their lives. Joseph was born on May 11, 1863, in Hocking County to Isaac and Mary (Delong) Bigham. He grew up in Laurel Township, and his father worked as a farmer. On Apr 3, 1886, he married Louisa Anna Hendrickson, daughter of George and Mary (Leisure) Hendrickson. Together they had four children: Samuel Edison, Metta (who died as an infant), Alvah Medred, and Goldie Theresa. Joseph's wife, Anna, remarried to Samuel Lutz on Oct. 6, 1898, and the children surely lived with them along with Samuel's daughter from a previous marriage. However, on Jan. 14, 1899, Anna passed away. Though we can't be sure of a reason, Joseph and Anna's children were spread out by the 1900 federal census. Samuel went to live with Anna's brother, Frank. Alvah went to live with Salem and Samantha Shoemaker, and worked as a servant. Goldie went to live with two of Anna's sisters, Mary and Lavina.

Oliver Benway was born in Canada on Dec. 20, 1861. By 1880, he was living in Antrim County, Michigan, with his brother William. Their father had passed away, but their mother, Louisa, was living with them. On Oct. 27, 1884, Oliver married Elizabeth Della Bigham in Michigan. According to his obituary, Louisa lost her life in a fire not long after his marriage, and Oliver and Elizabeth moved back to Hocking County. The time of this can gauged by the births of Oliver and Elizabeth's children. They had four daughters together: Lydia, Lauretta, Minnie, and Nettie. Minnie was born in Michigan in 1892, and Nettie was born in Good Hope Township in 1894, making the move probably in 1893 or early 1894. After Oliver's death, Elizabeth remarried to Andrew Roop, on Apr. 22, 1897, in Hocking County. Andrew adopted Elizabeth's four daughters, and he and Elizabeth had four sons of their own. The last of these sons was named Oliver.

More About Louisa Anna Hendrickson:
Burial: Pisgah Church Cemetery, Good Hope Township, Hocking County, Ohio
Cause Of Death: Hemorrhage of Lungs

Notes for Louisa Anna Hendrickson:
Buried beside her first husband, Joseph Bigham.

Birth date is from age at death on her death record.
----

xi.   Nelson Ignacius Bigham, son of Isaac Bigham and Mary Elizabeth Delong was born on 09 Feb 1866 in Hocking County, Ohio. He died on 14 Dec 1936 in Laurel Township, Hocking County, Ohio. He married Eliza Jane Friend, daughter of Lorenzo Corbin Friend and Hannah Elizabeth Odell on 17 Apr 1888 in Hocking

County, Ohio. She was born on 11 Sep 1868 in Hocking County, Ohio. She died on 02 May 1933 in Laurel Township, Hocking County, Ohio.

More About Nelson Ignacius Bigham:
Burial: 17 Dec 1936 in Fairview Methodist Church Cemetery, Good Hope Township, Hocking County, Ohio
Cause Of Death: Heart Disease
Occupation: Farmer

More About Eliza Jane Friend:
Burial: 05 May 1933 in Fairview Methodist Church Cemetery, Good Hope Township, Hocking County, Ohio

xii.   Nancy Margaret Bigham, daughter of Isaac Bigham and Mary Elizabeth Delong was born on 09 Feb 1867 in Laurel Township, Hocking County, Ohio. She died on 24 Sep 1870 in Laurel Townshiop, Hocking County, Ohio.

More About Nancy Margaret Bigham:
Burial: Betheny Church Cemetery, Hocking County,
Ohio Cause Of Death: Burned to Death

xiii.   Elizabeth Della Bigham, daughter of Isaac Bigham and Mary Elizabeth Delong was born on 11 Mar 1870 in Hocking County, Ohio. She died on 23 Aug 1952 in Rockbridge, Hocking County, Ohio. She married Oliver Benway on 27 Oct 1884 in Central Lake, Antrim County, Michigan. He was born on 27 Dec 1861 in Canada. He died on 24 Jul 1895 in Good Hope Township, Hocking County, Ohio. She married Andrew Martin Roop, son of Martin Roop and Elizabeth Springer on 22 Apr 1897 in Hocking County, Ohio. He was born on 19 Mar 1869 in Good Hope Township, Hocking County, Ohio. He died on 22 Nov 1950 in Rockbridge, Hocking County, Ohio.

More About Elizabeth Della Bigham:
Burial: 26 Aug 1952 in Fairview Memorial Gardens, Rockbridge, Hocking County, Ohio
Cause Of Death: Cerebral Hemorrhage

Notes for Oliver Benway:
Marriage record states he was born in New York.

Bigham and Benway
by Konrad Stump, contributing writer to The Logan Daily News.

In each of our family histories, there are stories we have heard that stick with us, a lot of the time because they involve something that isn't quite explained or understood. Sometimes they are mentioned in passing, and sometimes the stories are known but there are elements that have been told incorrectly. The descendants of Joseph Bigham and Oliver Benway may know something of the story of their deaths, but we'd all like an account of the stories that have been passed down in pieces.

It was Wednesday, July 24, 1895. It was about 9 a.m. At his home in the

Northwestern part of Laurel Township, near Cantwell Cliffs, Joseph Bigham had been digging a well. He was preparing to build a new house, having made the excavation for the cellar and starting work on this well. He was being assisted but his brother-in-law, Oliver Benway. The evening before, they fired a blast in the well in order to get fire to burn in it, but it didn't do any good. They left the house about seven o'clock on Wednesday morning to work on the well. Joseph went down in the well, but was overcome by carbonic acid gas, which at the time was commonly called well damp. He called to Oliver to pull him up, but was too affected by the gas to hold the rope. Oliver called out for help. Mary Yantes, who was staying with the Bighams at the time, and Joseph's wife Anna, came to assist. Oliver lowered himself into the well, fanning Joseph for a few minutes in an attempt to revive him, but soon felt himself being overcome by the gas. He called for the women to pull him up; they were able to get him up about 16 to 17 feet, but he was so overcome by the gas he fell back to the bottom of the well, which at the time was about 35 feet deep.

Mary ran to the nearest neighbors about a half-mile away, and a group of men came back with her to assist. Dan Kline went down in the well to retrieve the men, but only got about half way before the gas overcame him and he needed to be pulled out. They pumped air into the well by means of a windmill and sheet, and a burning sheaf of wheat was lowered into it. Dan went back down in the bucket, tied a rope around the bodies of Joseph and Oliver, and brought them up. They had been dead for some time, it having been over an hour since Oliver first called for help. Oliver's head was badly cut from when he'd fallen back into the well.

The funerals took place at Mt. Pisgah, with the Rev. Mather officiating. Mather's sermon was delivered outside, as the people who'd come to attend the funerals couldn't fit in the church. People who were there guessed the attendees numbered around one thousand.

Here is what I can tell you of their lives. Joseph was born on May 11, 1863, in Hocking County to Isaac and Mary (Delong) Bigham. He grew up in Laurel Township, and his father worked as a farmer. On Apr 3, 1886, he married Louisa Anna Hendrickson, daughter of George and Mary (Leisure) Hendrickson. Together they had four children: Samuel Edison, Metta (who died as an infant), Alvah Medred, and Goldie Theresa. Joseph's wife, Anna, remarried to Samuel Lutz on Oct. 6, 1898, and the children surely lived with them along with Samuel's daughter from a previous marriage. However, on Jan. 14, 1899, Anna passed away. Though we can't be sure of a reason, Joseph and Anna's children were spread out by the 1900 federal census. Samuel went to live with Anna's brother, Frank. Alvah went to live with Salem and Samantha Shoemaker, and worked as a servant. Goldie went to live with two of Anna's sisters, Mary and Lavina.

Oliver Benway was born in Canada on Dec. 20, 1861. By 1880, he was living in Antrim County, Michigan, with his brother William. Their father had passed away, but their mother, Louisa, was living with them. On Oct. 27, 1884, Oliver married Elizabeth Della Bigham in Michigan. According to his obituary, Louisa lost her life in a fire not long after his marriage, and Oliver and Elizabeth moved back to Hocking County. The time of this can gauged by the births of Oliver and Elizabeth's children. They had four daughters together: Lydia, Lauretta, Minnie, and Nettie. Minnie was born in Michigan in 1892, and Nettie was born in Good Hope Township in 1894, making the move probably in 1893 or early 1894. After Oliver's death, Elizabeth remarried to Andrew Roop, on Apr. 22, 1897, in Hocking County. Andrew adopted Elizabeth's four daughters, and he and Elizabeth had four sons of their own. The last of these sons was named Oliver.

More About Andrew Martin Roop:
Burial: 25 Nov 1950 in Fairview Memorial Gardens, Rockbridge, Hocking
County, Ohio

Generation 6

32.   **Robert Stewart** was born about 1764 in Augusta County, Virginia. He died in 1806 in Bath County, Virginia. He married **Catherine Aleshire**, daughter of Benedict Aleshire and Elizabeth Williams on 16 Jan 1798 in Bath County, Virginia.

33.   **Catherine Aleshire**, daughter of Benedict Aleshire and Elizabeth Williams was born in 1778 in Augusta County, Virginia. She died in Sep 1802 in Bath County, Virginia.

Notes for Catherine Aleshire:
Died in childbirth while delivering William.
Marriage record has Elshire for surname.

Catherine Aleshire and Robert Stewart had the following children:

     i.   Elizabeth Stewart, daughter of Robert Stewart and Catherine Aleshire was born on 03 Jan 1800 in Bath County, Virginia. She died on 04 Jan 1877 in Mason County, West Virginia. She married John Eckard. He was born about 1793 in Virginia. He died in Dec 1877 in Mason County, West Virginia.

More About Elizabeth Stewart:
Burial: Eckard-Jones Cemetery, Mason County, West Virginia

More About John Eckard:
Burial: Eckard-Jones Cemetery, Mason County, West Virginia
Occupation: 1850 in District 38, Mason County, Virginia; Farmer
Occupation: 1870 in Lewis Township, Mason County, West Virginia; Farmer

16.   ii. William Stewart, son of Robert Stewart and Catherine Aleshire was born on 09 Sep 1802 in Bath County, Virginia. He died on 16 Jul 1882 in Mason County, West Virginia. He married Martha Ann Van Sickle, daughter of Anthony Van Sickle and Rebecca Van Meter on 13 Sep 1823 in Mason County, Virginia. She was born on 15 Oct 1804 in Mason County, Virginia. She died on 02 Feb 1877 in Mason County, West Virginia.

34.   **Anthony Van Sickle**, son of Samuel Van Sickle and Sarah Thompson was born about 1770 in New Jersey. He died on 29 Sep 1815 in Mason County, Virginia. He married **Rebecca Van Meter**, daughter of Henry Van Meter and Martha Moore on 29 Apr 1789 in Green County, Pennsylvania.

35.   **Rebecca Van Meter**, daughter of Henry Van Meter and Martha Moore was born in Green County, Pennsylvania. She died on 28 Dec 1810 in Mason County, Virginia.

More About Anthony Van Sickle:
Burial: Point Pleasant, Virginia
Military Service: Mason County, Virginia; Captain of Anthony Van Sickle's Mason County Riflemen in War of 1812.

Rebecca Van Meter and Anthony Van Sickle had the following children:

    i.   Henry Van Sickle, son of Anthony Van Sickle and Rebecca Van Meter was born in 1793 in Green County, Pennsylvania. He died on 12 Nov 1863. He married Rachel Swan.

    ii.   Jesse Van Sickle, son of Anthony Van Sickle and Rebecca Van Meter was born in 1796 in Green County, Pennsylvania.

    iii.   Hannah Van Sickle, daughter of Anthony Van Sickle and Rebecca Van Meter was born in 1798 in Mason County, Virginia.

    iv.   Anthony Van Sickle, son of Anthony Van Sickle and Rebecca Van Meter was born in 1800 in Mason County, Virginia.

    v.   Abraham Van Sickle, son of Anthony Van Sickle and Rebecca Van Meter was born on 21 Oct 1802 in Mason County, Virginia. He died on 05 Feb 1873. He married Mary Riffle. She died after 21 Jun 1870.

More About Abraham Van Sickle:
Occupation: 1850 in District 38, Mason County, Virginia; Farmer
Occupation: 1860 in District 1, Mason County, Virginia; Farmer
Occupation: 1870 in Robinson Township, Mason County, West Virginia

    vi.   Samuel Van Sickle, son of Anthony Van Sickle and Rebecca Van Meter was born about 1803 in Virginia.

More About Samuel Van Sickle:
Occupation: 1880 in Robinson District, Mason County, West Virginia; Farmer

17.   vii. Martha Ann Van Sickle, daughter of Anthony Van Sickle and Rebecca Van Meter was born on 15 Oct 1804 in Mason County, Virginia. She died on 02 Feb 1877 in Mason County, West Virginia. She married William Stewart, son of Robert Stewart and Catherine Aleshire on 13 Sep 1823 in Mason County, Virginia. He was born on 09 Sep 1802 in Bath County, Virginia. He died on 16 Jul 1882 in Mason County, West Virginia.

    viii. John Van Sickle, son of Anthony Van Sickle and Rebecca Van Meter was born in 1807 in Mason County, Virginia.

    ix.   Joseph Van Sickle, son of Anthony Van Sickle and Rebecca Van Meter was born on 12 Feb 1809 in Mason County, Virginia. He died on 13 Aug 1884 in Farmington, St. Francois County, Missouri. He married Mary Mahala Hinkle, daughter of Gideon Hinkle and Rhoda Jane Allen on 26 Dec 1833. She was born about 1815. He married Sarah Rickert in 1836. She was born on 02 Nov 1816 in Virginia. She died on 16 Dec 1883 in Farmington, St. Francois County, Missouri.

More About Joseph Van Sickle:
Burial: 14 Aug 1884 in Farmington, St. Francois County, Missouri
Occupation: Minister

More About Sarah Rickert:
Burial: St. Francois County, Missouri

x.   Eli Van Sickle, son of Anthony Van Sickle and Rebecca Van Meter was born in 1810 in Mason County, Virginia.

38.   **Robert Johnson**. He married **Anna Greenlee**.

39.   **Anna Greenlee**, daughter of Edward Greenlee and Hannah Greenlee was born on 04 Jan 1795. She died on 30 Jun 1881 in Leon, West Virginia.

Anna Greenlee and Robert Johnson had the following children:

19.   i.   Hannah Johnson, daughter of Robert Johnson and Anna Greenlee was born in 1818 in Virginia. She died on 30 Nov 1870 in Mason County, West Virginia. She married Hutchinson McDaniel on 23 Mar 1833 in Mason County, Virginia. He was born on 04 Aug 1807 in Virginia. He died on 06 Jan 1875 in Mason County, West Virginia.

ii.   William Johnson.

iii.   Edward Johnson.

iv.   John Johnson.

v.   Mary Jane Johnson, daughter of Robert Johnson and Anna Greenlee was born on 25 Mar 1832 in Mason County, Virginia. She died about 1900 in Bible Grove, Missouri. She married William Guy Chapman, son of George Chapman and Lucinda Wilson on 20 Apr 1852 in Mason County, Virginia. He was born on 13 Dec 1829 in Mason County, Virginia. He died about 1903 in Bible Grove, Missouri.

vi.   Lewis Johnson.

vii.   Robert Johnson. He died on 03 Dec 1863.

viii.   David Johnson, son of Robert Johnson and Anna Greenlee was born on 26 Jun 1829.

40.   **William Casto** was born in 1784. He died in 1830. He married **Susanna Rollins**.

41.   **Susanna Rollins**.

Susanna Rollins and William Casto had the following children:

20.   i.   George R. Casto, son of William Casto and Susanna Rollins was born on 26 Jul 1826 in Virginia. He died on 04 Mar 1903 in Parchment Valley, Jackson County, West Virginia. He married Susanna Dewees, daughter of Samuel Dewees and Edith Battin on 12 Apr 1845 in Jackson County, Virginia. She was born on 20 Oct 1823 in Virginia. She died on 10 Sep 1859 in Jackson County, Virginia. He married Winifred (Winnie) Woodard, daughter of John Woodard and Mary Martin on 07 Nov 1861 in Parchment Valley, Jackson County, Virginia. She was born in Jan 1838 in Meigs County, Ohio. She died in 1910 in Ripley, Jackson County, West Virginia.

ii.   William Casto, son of William Casto and Susanna Rollins was born about 1822 in Virginia. He married Ann Dewees on 28 Dec 1841 in Jackson County, Virginia. She was born about 1825 in Virginia.

More About William Casto:
Occupation: 1850 in District 82, St. Louis, Missouri; Laborer
Occupation: 1860 in Jackson County, Virginia; Miller

42.   **Samuel Dewees** was born about 1785 in Pennsylvania. He died after 16 Jun 1860. He married **Edith Battin**.

43.   **Edith Battin** was born about 1878 in Pennsylvania. She died between 29 Aug 1850-16 Jun 1860.

More About Samuel Dewees:
Occupation: 1850 in District 27, Jackson County, Virginia; Farmer
Occupation: 1860 in Jackson County, Virginia; Farm Labor

Notes for Samuel Dewees:
Living two doors away from George R. Casto in 1850.

Edith Battin and Samuel Dewees had the following child:
21.   i. Susanna Dewees, daughter of Samuel Dewees and Edith Battin was born on 20 Oct 1823 in Virginia. She died on 10 Sep 1859 in Jackson County, Virginia. She married George R. Casto, son of William Casto and Susanna Rollins on 12 Apr 1845 in Jackson County, Virginia. He was born on 26 Jul 1826 in Virginia. He died on 04 Mar 1903 in Parchment Valley, Jackson County, West Virginia.

48.   **Henry William Tucker** was born on 27 Sep 1791 in Maryland. He died on 28 Jun 1863 in Carroll County, Ohio. He married **Anna Roby** on 10 Sep 1826 in Tuscarawas County, Ohio.

49.   **Anna Roby**. She died before 10 Sep 1848.

More About Henry William Tucker:
Burial: Leesville Cemetery, Leesville, Carroll County, Ohio
Living In: 1850 Orange Township, Carroll County, Ohio
Living In: 1860 Orange Township, Carroll County, Ohio
Military Service: War of 1812; Sergeant, Captain Cox's Company, Maryland Militia

Notes for Henry William Tucker:
Listed in Carroll County, Ohio records as a veteran of the War of 1812.

Birthdate is from headstone.

Anna Roby and Henry William Tucker had the following children:
i.   Hollis Tucker, son of Henry William Tucker and Anna Roby was born on 25 May 1830 in Leesburg, Carroll County, Ohio. He died on 28 Mar 1897 in Holton, Kansas. He married Sarah Ann McKeever, daughter of Clark McKeever and Jane Wallace on 20 Oct 1853 in Hocking County, Ohio. She was born on 20 Oct 1832 in Chester County, Pennsylvania. She died in 1909 in Holton, Kansas.

More About Hollis Tucker:
Occupation: 1850 in Lee Township, Athens County, Ohio; Student
Occupation: 1870 in Holton, Jackson County, Kansas; Dry Goods Merchant
Occupation: 1880 in Franklin Township, Jackson County, Kansas; Merchant
Military Service: Bet. 05 Feb-27 Aug 1864 in Civil War; Quarter Master Sergeant, Company I, 151st Ohio Infantry, U.S. Army

Notes for Hollis Tucker:
Mustered out of 151st Ohio Infantry at Camp Chase, Columbus, Ohio.

Hollis Tucker, one of the most prominent business men of our city, died at his residence on west Fourth Street, Sunday, March 28, 1897, aged 66 years, 10 months and 20 days. Hollis Tucker was born at Leesburg, Carrol County, Ohio, May 25, 1830. He was educated in the common schools of Ohio and at the academy of Albany, Ohio. In 1853 he married Miss Sarah A. McKeever, and in 1858 they came to Kansas, but returned to Ohio the same year. During the rebellion Mr. Tucker served in the 151st regiment, Co. I., O.V.I, as commissary sargeant. In his absence Mrs. Tucker kept the post office and took care of the little family. They again came to Kansas in 1865, locating in Holton in July of that year. In 1866 Mr. Tucker engaged in merchandising, which he has followed continuously to the present time. Mr. Tucker has been prominently connected with nearly every public enterprise that has benefitted and helped build up our city. In the contest of locating the county seat and building the courthouse he was one of the leaders. He perhaps did as much to secure the building of the Kansas Central railway to Holton as any other single man, and his labor and zeal was not less effectual in securing the Rock Island and Northwestern railroads. In building up Campbell University he has from the first stood shoulder to shoulder with the leaders of that enterprise, and for the past ten years has served as the president of the board of directors of that institution. Some four years ago on the death of County Treasurer George Lowell, Mr. Tucker was appointed to the office, and at the next general election he was elected to serve out Mr. Lowell's unexpired term, and also for a new term of two years, and it is generally conceded that the county never had a more competent, honest and faithful official. When his country needed his services as a soldier he left his store and post office to the care of his wife and went to the front as a private in the ranks. He leaves his wife and seven children living, H. C. Tucker, Miss Mary Rose, Misses Florence and Clara, of this place; Mack, in the employ of the Rock Island at Clyde; Sherd, train dispatcher on the Northwestern, and Will, engaged in mining in Colorado .
Personal. A. M. Tucker, of Clifton, Kan., and Sherd Tucker, of Kansas City, were called home the first of the week by the death of their father. The Holton Recorder, April 1, 1897.

More About Sarah Ann McKeever:
Living In: 1900 Holton, Jackson County, Kansas

Notes for Sarah Ann McKeever:
Obituary published in "The Holton Recorder" in Holton, Kansas on December 2, 1909.

 ii. W. L. Tucker, son of Henry William Tucker and Anna Roby was born about 1831.

24. iii. Wesley Summers Tucker, son of Henry William Tucker and Anna Roby was born on 03 Apr 1834 in Leesburg, Carroll County, Ohio. He died on 14 Aug 1906 in Goodhope Township, Hocking County, Ohio. He married Phebe Hutson, daughter of James Hutson and Ellenor Clark on 01 May 1856 in Hocking County, Ohio. She was born on 18 May 1834 in Carroll County, Ohio. She died on 18 Nov 1905 in Lancaster, Ohio.

 iv. William Henry Harrison Tucker, son of Henry William Tucker and Anna Roby was born on 08 May 1840 in Leesburg, Carroll County, Ohio. He died on 16 Feb 1904 in Bartlett Township, Todd County, Minnesota. He married Rebecca J. Russell, daughter of Samuel Russell and Caroline (unknown) on 07 Jul 1864 in Hocking County, Ohio. She was born on 18 Jul 1843 in Knox County, Ohio. She died on 28 Jan 1890.

More About William Henry Harrison Tucker:
Burial: Greenlawn Cemetery, Verndale, Wadena County,
Minnesota
Living In: 1875 Martinsburg, Knox County, Ohio
Living In: 1900 With his daughter, Constance, and her family in Bartlett Township, Todd County, Minnesota.
Occupation: 1860 in Orange Township, Carroll County, Ohio; Chair Maker
Occupation: 1870 in Bladensburg, Jackson Township, Knox County, Ohio; Painting
Occupation: 1880 in Pleasant Township, Knox County, Ohio; General Merchandise
Occupation: Chair Maker, Brick Layer, Merchant
Military Service: Bet. 12 Oct 1861-May 1864 in Civil War; Company K, 51st Ohio Infantry, U.S. Army

More About Rebecca J. Russell:
Burial: Greenlawn Cemetery, Verndale, Wadena County, Minnesota

50.   **James Hutson** was born about 1802 in Pennsylvania. He died on 17 Mar 1889 in Fox Township, Carroll County, Ohio. He married **Ellenor Clark**.

51.   **Ellenor Clark**, daughter of Nathan Clark and Elizabeth (unknown) was born about 1805 in Pennsylvania. She died between 28 Sep 1850-25 Nov 1852 in Ohio.

More About James Hutson:
Living In: Bet. 1840-1880 Fox Township, Carroll County, Ohio
Occupation: Farmer; Fox Township, Carroll County, Ohio

Notes for Ellenor Clark:
Death certificate of John C. Hutson gives her name as Ellen May.

Ellenor Clark and James Hutson had the following children:
        i.   Elizabeth Hutson, daughter of James Hutson and Ellenor Clark was born about 1832 in Ohio.

       ii.   John C. Hutson, son of James Hutson and Ellenor Clark was born on 26 Mar 1834 in Carroll County, Ohio. He died on 06 Aug 1921 in Fairfield Township, Columbiana County, Ohio. He married Martha Cross about 1858. She was born in 1838 in Ohio. She died in 1907 in Ohio.

               More About John C. Hutson:
               Burial: 09 Aug 1921 in Fairfield Cemetery, Fairfield Township, Columbiana County, Ohio
               Cause Of Death: Uremia
               Living In: 1900 Fairfield Township, Columbiana County, Ohio
               Occupation: Farmer

               Notes for John C. Hutson:

Death certificate gives March 26, 1834 as birth date. 1900 U.S. census gives February 1833 as birth date. Head Stone gives birth year as 1834.

More About Martha Cross:
Burial: Fairfield Cemetery, Fairfield Township, Columbiana County, Ohio

Notes for Martha Cross:
Birth date on head stone is 1838.

25.   iii. Phebe Hutson, daughter of James Hutson and Ellenor Clark was born on 18 May 1834 in Carroll County, Ohio. She died on 18 Nov 1905 in Lancaster, Ohio. She married Wesley Summers Tucker, son of Henry William Tucker and Anna Roby on 01 May 1856 in Hocking County, Ohio. He was born on 03 Apr 1834 in Leesburg, Carroll County, Ohio. He died on 14 Aug 1906 in Goodhope Township, Hocking County, Ohio.

iv.   Sarah Hutson, daughter of James Hutson and Ellenor Clark was born about 1835 in Ohio.

v.   Susannah Hutson, daughter of James Hutson and Ellenor Clark was born on 26 Jun 1836 in Ohio. She died on 03 Jan 1904 in Jefferson County, Ohio. She married John Parsons on 03 Jul 1855 in Carroll County, Ohio. He was born in Jul 1834 in Hammondsville, Jefferson County, Ohio. He died on 20 Mar 1905 in Salem Township, Jefferson County, Ohio.

vi.   Ellen Hutson, daughter of James Hutson and Ellenor Clark was born about 1840 in Ohio.

vii.   Lydia Hutson, daughter of James Hutson and Ellenor Clark was born about 1842 in Ohio.

viii.   Catherine Hutson, daughter of James Hutson and Ellenor Clark was born about 1844 in Ohio.

ix.   Rachael Hutson, daughter of James Hutson and Ellenor Clark was born about 1845 in Ohio.

x.   James S. Hutson, son of James Hutson and Ellenor Clark was born in 1846 in Ohio. He died in 1930 in Kansas. He married Rebecca Nestrick on 16 Nov 1871 in Carroll County, Ohio. She was born in 1844 in Ohio. She died in 1925 in Kansas.

More About James S. Hutson:
Burial: High Prairie Cemetery, Altoona, Wilson County, Kansas
Military Service: Civil War; 26th Independent Battery, Ohio Light Artillery

More About Rebecca Nestrick:
Burial: High Prairie Cemetery, Altoona, Wilson County, Kansas

52.   **John Fox** was born in Dec 1780 in Pennsylvania. He died on 28 Feb 1856 in Hocking County,

Ohio. He married **Nancy Julien** on 01 Apr 1806 in Fairfield County, Ohio.

53.   **Nancy Julien** was born on 21 Apr 1782 in Pennsylvania.

More About John Fox:
Burial: Mount Olive Cemetery, South Perry, Hocking County,
Ohio
Cause Of Death: Murdered by Elias Primmer

Nancy Julien and John Fox had the following children:

     i.   James Fox, son of John Fox and Nancy Julien was born on 06 Jun 1811 in Hocking County, Ohio. He died on 31 Mar 1887 in Laurel Township, Hocking County, Ohio. He married Nancy Clutter. She was born on 17 Jun 1817 in West Virginia. She died on 30 Jan 1898 in Laurel Township, Hocking County, Ohio.

          More About James Fox:
          Burial: Brown Cemetery, Goodhope Township, Hocking County, Ohio

          Notes for James Fox:
          Date of birth is from age at death on headstone.

          Death record has March 31, 1887 for date of death. Headstone has March 30, 1887 for date of death.

          More About Nancy Clutter:
          Burial: Brown Cemetery, Goodhope Township, Hocking County, Ohio

          Notes for Nancy Clutter:
          Death record has January 30, 1898 for date of death. Headstone has January 31, 1898 for date of death.
          ----

27.   ii. Peter Fox, son of John Fox and Nancy Julien was born on 06 Jan 1814 in Laurel Township, Hocking County, Ohio. He died on 08 Feb 1890 in Hocking County, Ohio. He married Deborah White, daughter of James White on 04 Mar 1838 in Perry County, Ohio. She was born on 14 Feb 1817 in Hocking County, Ohio. She died on 16 Jan 1900 in Hocking County, Ohio.

     iii.   William Fox.

54.   **James White**.

James White had the following child:

27.   i. Deborah White, daughter of James White was born on 14 Feb 1817 in Hocking County, Ohio. She died on 16 Jan 1900 in Hocking County, Ohio. She married Peter Fox, son of John Fox and Nancy Julien on 04 Mar 1838 in Perry County, Ohio. He was born on 06 Jan 1814 in Laurel Township, Hocking County, Ohio. He died on 08 Feb 1890 in Hocking County, Ohio.

56.   **John W. Davis**. He married **(Unknown)**.

57.   **(Unknown)**.

(Unknown) and John W. Davis had the following child:

28.   i. Levi Davis, son of John W. Davis and (Unknown) was born on 01 Jul 1805 in Loudoun County, Virginia. He died on 06 Jun 1885 in Falls Township, Hocking County, Ohio. He married Mary Ann Rodman on 15 Aug 1830 in Muskingum County, ohio. She was born about 1812 in Pennsylvania. She died on 01 Dec 1886 in Falls Township, Hocking County, Ohio.

60.   **Samuel Bigham**, son of William Bigham and Sarah Barton was born about 1800 in County Armagh, Ireland. He died on 31 Oct 1836 in Richland Township, Guernsey County, Ohio. He married **Sarah Morris**, daughter of Isaac Morris and Sarah McBurney on 08 Mar 1821 in Guernsey County, Ohio.

61.   **Sarah Morris**, daughter of Isaac Morris and Sarah McBurney was born on 20 Nov 1802 in Pennsylvania. She died on 30 Jun 1870 in Rockbridge, Hocking County, Ohio.

More About Samuel Bigham:
Burial: Old Washington Cemetery, Guernsey County,
Ohio Cause Of Death: Calomel Poisoning

More About Sarah Morris:
Burial: Brown Cemetery, Goodhope Township, Hocking County, Ohio

Sarah Morris and Samuel Bigham had the following children:

      i. Margaret Bigham, daughter of Samuel Bigham and Sarah Morris was born in 1822 in Guernsey County, Ohio. She died in 1883 in Hocking County, Ohio. She married John Botts on 10 Aug 1837 in Guernsey County, Ohio. He was born about 1815 in Ohio.

        More About John Botts:
        Occupation: 1850 in Good Hope Township, Hocking County, Ohio; Farmer
        Occupation: 1860 in Macon County, Illinois; Farmer

      ii. William Bigham, son of Samuel Bigham and Sarah Morris was born on 09 Dec 1825 in Guernsey County, Ohio. He died on 06 Mar 1896 in Kaufman County, Texas. He married Hannah Calistia Julian, daughter of Stephen Julian and Hannah Berry on 10 Aug 1848 in Fairfield County, Ohio. She was born on 27 Mar 1827 in Clear Creek Township, Fairfield County, Ohio. She died on 30 Aug 1872 in Illinois.

        More About William Bigham:
        Burial: Dry Creek Cemetery, Kaufman County, Texas
        Occupation: 1850 in Perry Township, Hocking County, Ohio; Carpenter
        Occupation: 1860 in Laurel Township, Hocking County, Ohio; Farmer
        Occupation: 1870 in Flat Branch, Shelby County, Illinois; House Carpenter
        Occupation: 1880 in Kaufman County, Texas; Farming

        More About Hannah Calistia Julian:
        Burial: Prairie Home Cemetery, Moweaqua, Shelby County, Illinois

31.   iii. Isaac Bigham, son of Samuel Bigham and Sarah Morris was born on 10 Mar 1828

in Guernsey County, Ohio. He died on 29 Nov 1896 in Laurel Township, Hocking County, Ohio. He married Mary Elizabeth Delong, daughter of Samuel Franklin Delong and Mary Ann Kimble on 16 Apr 1850 in Hocking County, Ohio. She was born on 19 Jan 1831 in Laurel Township, Hocking County, Ohio. She died on 30 Jun 1877 in Hocking County, Ohio. He married Sophia Julian, daughter of Eli Julian and Emeline Julian on 09 Apr 1879 in Hocking County, Ohio. She was born on 02 Oct 1840 in Hocking County, Ohio. She died on 06 Mar 1921 in Chico, California.

iv.   Abraham Bigham, son of Samuel Bigham and Sarah Morris was born on 30 Oct 1830 in Guernsey County, Ohio. He died on 11 Nov 1877 in Van Wert County, Ohio. He married Sarah Mann, daughter of James T. Mann and Caroline Worthman on 06 Feb 1851 in Hocking County, Ohio. She was born about Aug 1834 in Hocking County, Ohio. She died on 13 Feb 1884 in Van Wert County, Ohio.

More About Abraham Bigham:
Living In: 1850 With John Wittner and his family in Good Hope Township, Hocking County, Ohio.
Occupation: 1860 in Perry Township, Hocking County, Ohio; Farmer

More About Sarah Mann:
Living In: 1880 Next door to her parents in Washington Township, Van Wert County, Ohio.

Notes for Sarah Mann:
Age at death on death record is 49 years and 6 months.
----

62.   **Samuel Franklin Delong**, son of Abraham Delong and Johannah Steman was born about 1803 in Pennsylvania. He died after 20 Aug 1870 in Hocking County, Ohio. He married **Mary Ann Kimble** on 14 Aug 1825 in Laurel Township, Hocking County, Ohio.

63.   **Mary Ann Kimble** was born in 1805 in Fairfield County, Ohio. She died on 15 Nov 1862 in Hocking County, Ohio.

More About Samuel Franklin Delong:
Occupation: 1850 in Laurel Township, Hocking County, Ohio; Farmer
Occupation: 1860 in Laurel Township, Hocking County, Ohio; Farmer
Occupation: 1870 in Perry Township, Hocking County, Ohio; Post Master

Mary Ann Kimble and Samuel Franklin Delong had the following children:

i.   Solomon Delong, son of Samuel Franklin Delong and Mary Ann Kimble was born about 1826 in Laurel Township, Hocking County, Ohio. He married Mary Ellen Brown on 17 Oct 1844 in Fairfield County, Ohio. She was born about 1824 in Virginia. She died after 20 Jun 1900.

More About Solomon Delong:
Occupation: 1850 in Perry Township, Hocking County, Ohio; Farmer
Occupation: 1860 in Perry Township, Hocking County, Ohio; Farmer
Occupation: 1870 in Laurel Township, Hocking County, Ohio; Day Laborer

More About Mary Ellen Brown:

Living In: 1900 With her daughter, Louisa, and her family in Ridge Township, Shelby County, Illinois.

    ii.   John Delong, son of Samuel Franklin Delong and Mary Ann Kimble was born on 03 Apr 1829 in Laurel Township, Hocking County, Ohio. He died on 21 Feb 1884 in Givens, Pike County, Ohio. He married Mary Fox on 24 Nov 1850 in Hocking County, Ohio. She was born on 26 Apr 1835 in Ohio. She died on 05 Nov 1852. He married Delilah Van Curen on 03 Jul 1853 in Hocking County, Ohio. She was born in Sep 1833 in Ohio. She died after 08 Jun 1900.

More About John Delong:
Burial: Givens Chapel Cemetery, Givens, Pike County, Ohio
Occupation: 1860 in Madison Township, Fairfield County, Ohio; Farmer
Occupation: 1870 in Madison Township, Fairfield County, Ohio; Farm Laborer
Occupation: 1880 in Circleville Township, Pickaway County, Ohio; Laborer
Military Service: Civil War; Company D, 58th Ohio Infantry

More About Mary Fox:
Burial: Brown Cemetery, Goodhope Township, Hocking County, Ohio

More About Delilah Van Curen:
Living In: 1900 With her daughter, Elizabeth, and her family in Johnson Township, Champaign County, Ohio.

31.   iii. Mary Elizabeth Delong, daughter of Samuel Franklin Delong and Mary Ann Kimble was born on 19 Jan 1831 in Laurel Township, Hocking County, Ohio. She died on 30 Jun 1877 in Hocking County, Ohio. She married Isaac Bigham, son of Samuel Bigham and Sarah Morris on 16 Apr 1850 in Hocking County, Ohio. He was born on 10 Mar 1828 in Guernsey County, Ohio. He died on 29 Nov 1896 in Laurel Township, Hocking County, Ohio.

    iv. Samuel Jackson Delong, son of Samuel Franklin Delong and Mary Ann Kimble was born in 1833 in Laurel Township, Hocking County, Ohio. He died on 25 May 1864 in Georgia. He married Nancy McCaslin on 06 Mar 1856 in Hocking County, Ohio. She was born in Ohio.

More About Samuel Jackson Delong:
Living In: 1863 Madison Township, Fairfield County, Ohio
Occupation: 1860 in Madison Township, Fairfield County, Ohio; Day Laborer Military Service: Bet. 31 Mar-25 May 1864 ; Company I, 73rd Ohio Infantry, U.S.A.

Notes for Samuel Jackson Delong:
Killed in action May 25, 1864 during the battle of New Hope Church in Georgia.
----

    v.   Josiah Delong, son of Samuel Franklin Delong and Mary Ann Kimble was born on 4 Jan 1835 in Laurel Township, Hocking County, Ohio. He died on 24 Sep 1916 in Perkins Township, Erie County, Ohio. He married Mary Elizabeth Julien, daughter of Alexander Julien and Elenor Clendenin on 05 Nov 1857 in Hocking County, Ohio. She was born on 13 Mar 1840 in Ohio. She died on 19 Mar 1880 in Ohio. He married Mary Caroline Waltner on 07 Oct 1880 in Putnam County, Ohio. He married

Mary J. Wells on 30 Nov 1884 in Fairfield County, Ohio. She was born in 1858.
She died in 1897. He married Frances Clara Shank, daughter of John Shank and
Fannie Everette on 29 Mar 1900 in Hocking County, Ohio. She was born on 19
Jan 1846 in South Perry, Hocking County, Ohio. She died on 17 Sep 1936 in
Perry Township, Hocking County, Ohio.

More About Josiah Delong:
Burial: 25 Sep 1916 in Elmwood Cemetery, Lancaster, Fairfield County,
Ohio
Living In: 1890 Columbus Grove, Putnam County, Ohio
Occupation: 1860 in Madison Township, Fairfield County, Ohio; Day Laborer
Occupation: 1870 in Amanda Township, Fairfield County, Ohio; Farm
Laborer
Occupation: 1880 in Columbus Grove, Putnam County, Ohio; Day Laborer
Occupation: 1900 in Worthington, Franklin County, Ohio; Farmer
Occupation: 1910 in Greenfield Township, Fairfield County, Ohio; Farm
Laborer, Odd Jobs
Military Service: Bet. 28 Feb 1864-10 May 1865; Company B, 31st Ohio
Infantry, U.S. Army

Notes for Josiah Delong:
Mustered out of Company B, 31st Ohio Infantry on May 10, 1865 at
Camp Dennison, Ohio.

Died at State Soldiers Home.

More About Mary Elizabeth Julien:
Burial: Bogart Cemetery, Columbus Grove, Putnam County, Ohio

More About Frances Clara Shank:
Burial: 30 Sep 1936 in Betheny Church Cemetery, Perry Township,
Hocking County, Ohio
Living In: 1930 With her brother, William Shank, in Perry Township, Hocking
County, Ohio.

Notes for Frances Clara Shank:
Name and birthdate are on headstone with Josiah Delong in Elmwood
Cemetery, Lancaster, Ohio but she is buried in Betheny Cemetery, Perry
Township, Hocking County, Ohio.
----

vi.   Eveline Delong, daughter of Samuel Franklin Delong and Mary Ann Kimble was
       born on 02 Nov 1836 in Laurel Township, Hocking County, Ohio. She died on 09
       Jul 1909 in Lancaster, Fairfield County, Ohio. She married Sampson Friend, son
       of George Friend and Sarah (unknown) on 30 Dec 1854 in Hocking County, Ohio.
       He was born on 23 Apr 1834 in Ohio. He died in 1896 in Ohio.

       More About Eveline Delong:
       Burial: Forest Rose Cemetery, Lancaster, Fairfield County,

       Ohio More About Sampson Friend:

Burial: Forest Rose Cemetery, Lancaster, Fairfield County,
Ohio Living In: 1890 Lancaster, Fairfield County, Ohio
Occupation: 1860 in Perry Township, Hocking County, Ohio; Laborer
Occupation: 1870 in Clear Creek Township, Fairfield County, Ohio; Farm
Laborer
Occupation: 1880 in Hocking Township, Fairfield County, Ohio; Laborer
Military Service: Bet. 24 Jun 1864-19 Jun 1865; Company I, 122nd Ohio
Infantry, U.S.A.

Notes for Sampson Friend:
Mustered out of U.S. Army on June 19, 1865 at Washington D.C.
----

vii.   Joseph Delong, son of Samuel Franklin Delong and Mary Ann Kimble was born
on 23 Apr 1839 in Laurel Township, Hocking County, Ohio. He died on 09 Dec
1891 in Goodhope Township, Hocking County, Ohio. He married Catherine Woltz,
daughter of Thomas Woltz and Nancy Sutton on 01 Dec 1859 in Hocking County,
Ohio. She was born on 03 Jul 1839 in Hocking County, Ohio. She died on 12 Dec
1929 in Lancaster, Fairfield County, Ohio.

More About Joseph Delong:
Occupation: 1860 in Laurel Township, Hocking County, Ohio; Farmer
Occupation: 1870 in Clear Creek Township, Fairfield County, Ohio; Farm
Laborer
Occupation: 1880 in Hocking Township, Fairfield County, Ohio; Farmer

More About Catherine Woltz:
Burial: 14 Dec 1929 in Fairview Methodist Church Cemetery, Good Hope
Township, Hocking County, Ohio
Living In: 1900 Good Hope Township, Hocking County, Ohio
Living In: 1910 With her daughter, Alice, and her family in Good Hope Township,
Hocking County, Ohio.
Living In: 1920 With her daughter, Alice, and her family in Good Hope Township,
Hocking County, Ohio.

viii.   Calista Ann Delong, daughter of Samuel Franklin Delong and Mary Ann Kimble
was born on 01 Nov 1841 in Laurel Township, Hocking County, Ohio. She died on
07 Aug 1901 in Ohio. She married John F. Thompson. She married Maurice Kane
on 17 Jun 1860 in Hocking County, Ohio. He was born on 23 Jul 1819 in Fairfield
County, Ohio. He died on 02 Dec 1879 in Perry Township, Hocking County, Ohio.
She married John Roth between 15 Jun 1880-16 Mar 1884. He died before 23 Jun
1900.

More About Calista Ann Delong:
Burial: Betheny Cemetery, Buena Vista, Hocking County, Ohio
Living In: 1880 Perry Township, Hocking County, Ohio
Living In: 1900 With her son, George, and his family in Madison Township,
Fairfield County, Ohio.

More About John F. Thompson and Calista Ann Delong:
Marriage License: 14 Dec 1858 in Hocking County, Ohio

Marriage Fact: Marriage license returned marked "annuled December 21, 1858".

More About Maurice Kane:
Burial: Betheny Cemetery, Buena Vista, Hocking County, Ohio
Cause Of Death: Consumption

Notes for Maurice Kane:
Headstone has 60 years, 4 months and 9 days for age at death. Death record
has 60 years, 4 months and 28 days for age at death.
----

ix.   Malinda Delong, daughter of Samuel Franklin Delong and Mary Ann Kimble was born
        on 26 Mar 1844 in Laurel Township, Hocking County, Ohio. She died on 12 Jun 1920
        in Wyandotte, Wayne County, Michigan. She married Louis L. Smyers, son of John
        Smyers on 03 Mar 1864 in Hocking County, Ohio. He was born on 23 Feb 1832 in
        Ohio. He died on 09 Sep 1915 in Wyandotte, Wayne County, Michigan.

        More About Malinda Delong:
        Burial: 15 Jun 1920 in Ferndale Cemetery, Riverview, Wayne County, Michigan

        Notes for Malinda Delong:
        Buried with her daughter, Ida, and Ida's husband. All three names are on the
        same headstone.

        1841 is year of birth on headstone.

        More About Louis L. Smyers:
        Burial: Lancaster, Ohio
        Occupation: 1870 in Perry Township, Hocking County, Ohio; Common Labor
        Occupation: 1880 in Madison Township, Fairfield County, Ohio; Farm Laborer
        Occupation: 1900 in Madison Township, Fairfield County, Ohio; Farmer
        Occupation: 1910 in Madison Township, Fairfield County, Ohio; Retired
        Military Service: Bet. 09 Aug 1861-20 Jul 1865 in Civil War; Company B, 31st
        Ohio Infantry, U.S. Army

        Notes for Louis L. Smyers:
        Mustered out of Company B, 31st Ohio infantry on July 20, 1865 at
        Louisville, Kentucky.

        ----

x.   James Delong, son of Samuel Franklin Delong and Mary Ann Kimble was born on
        6 Jan 1847 in Laurel Township, Hocking County, Ohio. He died on 04 Mar 1912 in
        Pleasant Township, Fairfield County, Ohio. He married Adian Ann Cave, daughter of
        Michael Cave and Sarah Moore on 05 Jan 1867 in Hocking County, Ohio. She was
        born in Jun 1847 in Ohio. She died on 25 Dec 1933 in Derby, Darby Township,
        Pickaway County, Ohio. He married Margaretta Kane, daughter of Maurice Kane and
        Elizabeth McDowell on 08 Mar 1874 in Fairfield County, Ohio. She was born on
        7 Feb 1852 in Hocking County, Ohio. She died on 09 Jul 1938 in Lancaster,

Fairfield County, Ohio.

More About James Delong:
Burial: 07 Mar 1912 in Saint Mathews Cemetery, Fairfield County, Ohio
Living In: 1870 With his brother, Joseph, and his family in Clear Creek Township,
Fairfield County, Ohio.
Occupation: 1870 in Clear Creek Township, Fairfield County, Ohio; Farm
Laborer
Occupation: 1880 in Amanda Township, Fairfield County, Ohio; Laborer
Occupation: 1900 in Pleasant Township, Fairfield County, Ohio; Laborer
Occupation: 1910 in Pleasant Township, Fairfield County, Ohio; None

More About Adian Ann Cave:
Burial:
Burial: Pleasant Cemetery, Mount Sterling, Madison County, Ohio

More About Margaretta Kane:
Burial: 13 Jul 1938 in Saint Mathews Cemetery, Fairfield County, Ohio
Living In: 1920 Lancaster, Fairfield County, Ohio
Living In: 1930 Lancaster, Fairfield County, Ohio

    xi.   Minerva Jane Delong, daughter of Samuel Franklin Delong and Mary Ann Kimble
was born on 19 Mar 1852 in Laurel Township, Hocking County, Ohio. She died on
2 Oct 1915 in Lancaster, Fairfield County, Ohio. She married James Raymond on
29 Nov 1868 in Hocking County, Ohio. He was born about 1847 in Ohio.
She married Elias Potts on 23 Oct 1877 in Fairfield County, Ohio.

More About Minerva Jane Delong:
Burial: Amanda Township Cemetery, Amanda, Fairfield County, Ohio

More About James Raymond:
Living In: 1860 With Caleb Hedges and his family in Perry Township, Hocking
County, Ohio.
Occupation: 1870 in Laurel Township, Hocking County, Ohio; Farm Laborer

---

Generation 7

66.   **Benedict Aleshire** was born in 1751 in Virginia. He died in Mason County, Virginia. He married
Elizabeth Williams.

67.   **Elizabeth Williams** was born in Virginia. She died in Mason County, Virginia.

Elizabeth Williams and Benedict Aleshire had the following children:

33.   i. Catherine Aleshire, daughter of Benedict Aleshire and Elizabeth Williams was born in
1778 in Augusta County, Virginia. She died in Sep 1802 in Bath County, Virginia. She
married Robert Stewart on 16 Jan 1798 in Bath County, Virginia. He was born about
1764 in Augusta County, Virginia. He died in 1806 in Bath County, Virginia.

    ii.   Elizabeth Aleshire.

    iii.   Sarah Aleshire.

iv.   Lucretia Aleshire.

v.   Margaret Aleshire, daughter of Benedict Aleshire and Elizabeth Williams was born in 1784 in Bath County, Virginia. She died in 1850 in Mason County, Virginia.

vi.   Sophia Aleshire.

vii.   Susanna Aleshire, daughter of Benedict Aleshire and Elizabeth Williams was born on 14 Feb 1787 in Virginia. She died on 02 Oct 1865 in Mason County, West Virginia. She married John Greenlee on 19 Feb 1809 in Mason County, Virginia.

viii.   Jacob Aleshire, son of Benedict Aleshire and Elizabeth Williams was born in 1788 in Virginia. He died on 31 Dec 1877 in Mason County, Virginia.

68.   **Samuel Van Sickle**. He married **Sarah Thompson**.

69.   **Sarah Thompson**.

Sarah Thompson and Samuel Van Sickle had the following children:

34.   i. Anthony Van Sickle, son of Samuel Van Sickle and Sarah Thompson was born about 1770 in New Jersey. He died on 29 Sep 1815 in Mason County, Virginia. He married Rebecca Van Meter, daughter of Henry Van Meter and Martha Moore on 29 Apr 1789 in Green County, Pennsylvania. She was born in Green County, Pennsylvania. She died on 28 Dec 1810 in Mason County, Virginia. He married Zilpha Hubbell, daughter of Abijah Hubbell on 06 Jun 1811 in Gallia County, Ohio. She died on 21 Nov 1857 in Meigs County, Ohio.

ii.   Zachariah Van Sickle.

iii.   Rebecca Van Sickle.

iv.   Christine Van Sickle, daughter of Samuel Van Sickle and Sarah Thompson was born in Pennsylvania. She died in Mason County, Virginia. She married Henry Van Meter. He was born in Jun 1773 in Pennsylvania. He died on 13 Dec 1857 in Mason County, Virginia.

70.   **Henry Van Meter**. He died in 1803 in Pennsylvania. He married **Martha Moore**.

71.   **Martha Moore** was born in 1730 in Maryland. She died in 1825 in Pennsylvania.

Martha Moore and Henry Van Meter had the following children:

i.   Jesse Van Meter. She died on 07 Oct 1787 in Pennsylvania.

ii.   Joseph Van Meter. He died in 1808.

iii.   Mary Van Meter.

35.   iv. Rebecca Van Meter, daughter of Henry Van Meter and Martha Moore was born in Green County, Pennsylvania. She died on 28 Dec 1810 in Mason County, Virginia. She married Anthony Van Sickle, son of Samuel Van Sickle and Sarah Thompson on 29 Apr 1789 in Green County, Pennsylvania. He was born about 1770 in New Jersey. He died on 29 Sep 1815 in Mason County, Virginia.

v.   Rachel Van Meter, daughter of Henry Van Meter and Martha Moore was born in 1751 in Pennsylvania.

vi.   Martha Van Meter, daughter of Henry Van Meter and Martha Moore was born on 24

Dec 1754 in Pennsylvania. She died on 24 Oct 1836 in Pennsylvania.

    vii. Alice Van Meter, daughter of Henry Van Meter and Martha Moore was born on 12 Feb 1756 in Chester, Pennsylvania. She died on 12 Sep 1839 in Ohio.

    viii. Sarah Van Meter, daughter of Henry Van Meter and Martha Moore was born on 24 Jun 1758 in Pennsylvania. She died on 12 Sep 1839 in Pennsylvania.

    ix. Elizabeth Van Meter, daughter of Henry Van Meter and Martha Moore was born in 1761 in Virginia. She died in 1802.

    x. Absolom Van Meter, son of Henry Van Meter and Martha Moore was born in 1765 in Virginia. He died in 1803 in Mason County, Virginia.

    xi. John Van Meter, son of Henry Van Meter and Martha Moore was born in 1769 in Virginia. He died in 1812 in Mason County, Virginia.

    xii. Phoebe Van Meter, daughter of Henry Van Meter and Martha Moore was born on 8 Jul 1770 in Virginia. She died on 14 Feb 1853.

    xiii. Henry Van Meter, son of Henry Van Meter and Martha Moore was born in Jun 1773 in Pennsylvania. He died on 13 Dec 1857 in Mason County, Virginia. He married Christine Van Sickle. She was born in Pennsylvania. She died in Mason County, Virginia.

78. **Edward Greenlee** was born on 08 Sep 1761 in Ulster, Ireland. He died on 23 Aug 1839 in Mason County, Virginia. He married **Hannah Greenlee**, daughter of Alexander Greenlee and Anna Henry on 13 Jul 1792 in Virginia.

79. **Hannah Greenlee**, daughter of Alexander Greenlee and Anna Henry was born on 26 Aug 1773. She died on 23 Feb 1865 in Mason County, West Virginia.

Hannah Greenlee and Edward Greenlee had the following children:

    i. David Greenlee.

    ii. Samuel Greenlee, son of Edward Greenlee and Hannah Greenlee was born on 20 Sep 1793 in Mason County, Virginia.

40.   iii. Anna Greenlee, daughter of Edward Greenlee and Hannah Greenlee was born on 4 Jan 1795. She died on 30 Jun 1881 in Leon, West Virginia. She married Robert Johnson.

    iv. William Greenlee, son of Edward Greenlee and Hannah Greenlee was born in 1797.

    v. Alexander Greenlee, son of Edward Greenlee and Hannah Greenlee was born on 28 Mar 1798.

    vi. Edward Greenlee, son of Edward Greenlee and Hannah Greenlee was born on 10 Jan 1801 in Leon, Mason County, Virginia. He died on 26 Jan 1874 in Leon, Mason County, West Virginia.

    vii. James Greenlee, son of Edward Greenlee and Hannah Greenlee was born on 01 Jan 1803.

    viii. Robert Greenlee, son of Edward Greenlee and Hannah Greenlee was born on 10

Nov 1805.

    ix.   Francis Greenlee, son of Edward Greenlee and Hannah Greenlee was born on 29 Oct 1808 in Mason County, Virginia. He died on 23 Mar 1889 in West Virginia.

    x.   Eastham Greenlee, son of Edward Greenlee and Hannah Greenlee was born on 12 Jan 1811.

    xi.   Rachel Greenlee, daughter of Edward Greenlee and Hannah Greenlee was born on 26 Aug 1813. She died on 16 Apr 1878.

102.   **Nathan Clark** was born in 1780 in Pennsylvania. He died on 25 Sep 1840 in Augusta Township, Carroll County, Ohio. He married **Elizabeth (unknown)**.

103.   **Elizabeth (unknown)** was born about 1786 in Pennsylvania. She died in 1836 in Augusta Township, Carroll County, Ohio.

Elizabeth (unknown) and Nathan Clark had the following children:

    i.   Sarah Clark, daughter of Nathan Clark and Elizabeth (unknown) was born in 1803 in Pennsylvania. She died in 1864.

52.   ii. Ellenor Clark, daughter of Nathan Clark and Elizabeth (unknown) was born about 1805 in Pennsylvania. She died between 28 Sep 1850-25 Nov 1852 in Ohio. She married James Hutson. He was born about 1802 in Pennsylvania. He died on 17 Mar 1889 in Fox Township, Carroll County, Ohio.

    iii. Priscilla Clark, daughter of Nathan Clark and Elizabeth (unknown) was born in 1806 in Pennsylvania. She died in 1860.

    iv. Elizabeth Clark, daughter of Nathan Clark and Elizabeth (unknown) was born in 1808 in Pennsylvania.

    v.   Hannah Clark, daughter of Nathan Clark and Elizabeth (unknown) was born in 1811 in Pennsylvania. She died in 1845.

    vi. Leah Clark, daughter of Nathan Clark and Elizabeth (unknown) was born in 1812 in Pennsylvania.

    vii. John S. Clark, son of Nathan Clark and Elizabeth (unknown) was born in 1813 in Pennsylvania. He died on 03 Mar 1888 in Augusta Township, Carroll County, Ohio.

      More About John S. Clark:
      Occupation: Farmer

    viii. Nathan Clark, son of Nathan Clark and Elizabeth (unknown) was born in 1816 in Pennsylvania. He died on 20 Jun 1876 in West Township, Columbiana County, Ohio.

      More About Nathan Clark:
      Occupation: Farmer

    ix. Ann Clark, daughter of Nathan Clark and Elizabeth (unknown) was born in 1821. She died in 1903.

x.   Mary Clark, daughter of Nathan Clark and Elizabeth (unknown) was born in 1822.

xi.   Rachel Clark, daughter of Nathan Clark and Elizabeth (unknown) was born in 1823.

xii.   Michael Clark, son of Nathan Clark and Elizabeth (unknown) was born in 1826 in Augusta Township, Carroll County, Ohio. He died in Nov 1894 in Augusta Township, Carroll County, Ohio.

More About Michael Clark:
Occupation: Farmer

xiii.   Jacob Clark, son of Nathan Clark and Elizabeth (unknown) was born in 1828.

xiv.   Allen P. Clark, son of Nathan Clark and Elizabeth (unknown) was born in 1831 in Carroll County, Ohio. He died on 27 Dec 1896 in West Township, Columbiana County, Ohio.

More About Allen P. Clark:
Occupation: Farmer

xv.   James Clark, son of Nathan Clark and Elizabeth (unknown) was born in 1833 in Ohio.

xvi.   Esau Clark, son of Nathan Clark and Elizabeth (unknown) was born in 1834 in Ohio.

120.   **William Bigham** was born in 1760 in County Armagh, Ireland. He died in 1844 in Wills Township, Guernsey County, Ohio. He married **Sarah Barton**.

121.   **Sarah Barton** was born in 1765 in Ireland. She died on 05 Oct 1826 in Wills Township, Guernsey County, Ohio.

More About William Bigham:
Burial: Old Washington Cemetery, Old Washington, Guernsey County, Ohio

More About Sarah Barton:
Burial: Old Washington Cemetery, Old Washington, Guernsey County, Ohio

Sarah Barton and William Bigham had the following children:

i.   James W. Bigham, son of William Bigham and Sarah Barton was born in 1784 in Ireland. He died in 1842 in Guernsey County, Ohio. He married Elizabeth McCreary on 26 Mar 1818.

61.   ii. Samuel Bigham, son of William Bigham and Sarah Barton was born about 1800 in County Armagh, Ireland. He died on 31 Oct 1836 in Richland Township, Guernsey County, Ohio. He married Sarah Morris, daughter of Isaac Morris and Sarah McBurney on 08 Mar 1821 in Guernsey County, Ohio. She was born on 20 Nov 1802 in Pennsylvania. She died on 30 Jun 1870 in Rockbridge, Hocking County, Ohio.

iii.   Jane Bigham, daughter of William Bigham and Sarah Barton was born on 11 Jun 1801 in Ireland. She died on 29 Sep 1865 in Wills Township, Guernsey County, Ohio. She married William B. Stewart on 09 Sep 1843 in Guernsey County, Ohio.

More About Jane Bigham:
Burial: Old Washington Cemetery, Old Washington, Guernsey County, Ohio

iv.   Sarah Bigham, daughter of William Bigham and Sarah Barton was born on 25 Mar 1803 in Ireland. She died on 15 Dec 1846 in Washington Township, Guernsey County, Ohio. She married James Clarke in Mar 1845 in Guernsey County, Ohio. He was born in 1796. He died in 1879.

More About Sarah Bigham:
Burial: Old Washington Cemetery, Old Washington, Guernsey County, Ohio

v.   Margaret Bigham, daughter of William Bigham and Sarah Barton was born in 1806. She married Isaac Warden on 13 Jan 1824 in Guernsey County, Ohio. He was born in 1794. He died in 1866 in Guernsey County, Ohio.

vi.   Rebecca Bigham, daughter of William Bigham and Sarah Barton was born in 1808.

vii.   William Bigham, son of William Bigham and Sarah Barton was born in 1810.

122.   **Isaac Morris** was born on 01 Jul 1777 in Philadelphia, Pennsylvania. He died on 02 Mar 1851 in Hocking County, Ohio. He married **Sarah McBurney** in 1798 in Pennsylvania.

123.   **Sarah McBurney** was born in 1781. She died on 30 Jun 1840 in Hocking County, Ohio.

More About Isaac Morris:
Burial: Brown Cemetery, Goodhope Township, Hocking County, Ohio

Sarah McBurney and Isaac Morris had the following children:

i.   Enoch Morris. He married Nancy Closser.

62.   ii. Sarah Morris, daughter of Isaac Morris and Sarah McBurney was born on 20 Nov 1802 in Pennsylvania. She died on 30 Jun 1870 in Rockbridge, Hocking County, Ohio. She married Samuel Bigham, son of William Bigham and Sarah Barton on 08 Mar 1821 in Guernsey County, Ohio. He was born about 1800 in County Armagh, Ireland. He died on 31 Oct 1836 in Richland Township, Guernsey County, Ohio. She married Edward Potter, son of Eli Potter and Martha Davenport on 06 Sep 1839 in Hocking County, Ohio. He was born about 1796 in Connecticutt. He died after 02 Aug 1870 in Ohio.

iii.   Nancy Morris, daughter of Isaac Morris and Sarah McBurney was born about 1804 in Pennsylvania. She married Joseph Frazee on 21 Feb 1826 in Belmont County, Ohio.

iv.   William Morris, son of Isaac Morris and Sarah McBurney was born about 1806 in Pennsylvania. He married Rebecca Thomas on 08 Aug 1830 in Belmont County, Ohio. She was born about 1810. She died in Virginia.

v.   Abraham Morris, son of Isaac Morris and Sarah McBurney was born on 20 May 1809 in Pennsylvania. He died on 17 Aug 1862 in Hocking County, Ohio. He married Sarah Hazlett on 02 Aug 1832 in Hocking County, Ohio. She was born on 22 May 1812 in Pennsylvania. She died on 18 Jan 1894 in Hocking County, Ohio.

vi.   Isaac Morris, son of Isaac Morris and Sarah McBurney was born about 1811 in Pennsylvania. He died before Dec 1854 in Hocking County, Ohio. He married

Abavilla Botts, daughter of John Botts and Sarah Haines on 21 Sep 1834 in Guernsey County, Ohio. She was born about 1814 in Ohio.

124. **Abraham Delong**, son of Henry Delong was born on 01 Jan 1773 in Pennsylvania. He died on 03 Nov 1859 in Allen County, Ohio. He married **Johannah Steman**, daughter of Christian Steman and Hannah Barr in Fayette County, Pennsylvania.

125. **Johannah Steman**, daughter of Christian Steman and Hannah Barr was born on 10 May 1788 in Rockingham County, Virginia. She died in 1875 in Allen County, Ohio.

More About Abraham Delong:
Occupation: 1850 in Marion Township, Hocking County, Ohio; Farmer

More About Johannah Steman:
Living In: 1860 With her son, Isaac, and his family in Logan Township, Auglaize County, Ohio.
Living In: 1870 With her son, Isaac, and his family in German Township, Allen County, Ohio.

Johannah Steman and Abraham Delong had the following children:

62.   i. Samuel Franklin Delong, son of Abraham Delong and Johannah Steman was born about 1803 in Pennsylvania. He died after 20 Aug 1870 in Hocking County, Ohio. He married Mary Ann Kimble on 14 Aug 1825 in Laurel Township, Hocking County, Ohio. She was born in 1805 in Fairfield County, Ohio. She died on 15 Nov 1862 in Hocking County, Ohio. He married Elizabeth Sterns, daughter of John Sterns and Mary (unknown) on 02 Mar 1865 in Hocking County, Ohio. She was born about 1816 in Pennsylvania. She died on 22 Dec 1891 in Columbus, Franklin County, Ohio.

    ii. Margaret Delong, daughter of Abraham Delong and Johannah Steman was born about 1809 in Pennsylvania.

      More About Margaret Delong:
Living In: 1850 With her parents in Marion Township, Hocking County, Ohio.
Living In: 1860 With her brother, Isaac, and his family in Logan Township, Auglaize County, Ohio.
Living In: 1870 With her brother, Isaac, and his family in German Township, Allen County, Ohio.

    iii. John Delong, son of Abraham Delong and Johannah Steman was born about 1811 in Pennsylvania. He married Mary Magdalene Spohn on 03 Jun 1834 in Fairfield County, Ohio. She was born about 1812 in Ohio.

      More About John Delong:
Occupation: 1850 in Marion Township, Hocking County, Ohio; Farmer

    iv. Christian Delong, son of Abraham Delong and Johannah Steman was born about 1813 in Ohio. He married Hannah Beery on 20 Mar 1845 in Fairfield County, Ohio. She was born about 1810 in Virginia.

      More About Christian Delong:
Occupation: 1850 in Marion Township, Hocking County, Ohio; Farmer

    v. Catherine Delong, daughter of Abraham Delong and Johannah Steman was born on 20 Apr 1816 in Ohio. She died on 30 Oct 1893 in Duchouquet Township,

Auglaize County, Ohio. She married Samuel Moyer on 17 Jan 1837 in Allen County, Ohio. He was born on 10 Jul 1813 in Ohio. He died on 22 Jan 1905 in Duchouquet Township, Auglaize County, Ohio.

More About Catherine Delong:
Burial: Saint Matthew Cemetery, Lima, Allen County, Ohio

More About Samuel Moyer:
Burial: Saint Matthew Cemetery, Lima, Allen County, Ohio

vi. Daniel Delong, son of Abraham Delong and Johannah Steman was born about 1818 in Ohio. He died after 08 Jun 1880. He married Nancy Reed on 11 Aug 1839 in Fairfield County, Ohio. She was born about 1820 in Ohio. He married Hannah Caffitz on 22 Aug 1869 in Fairfield County, Ohio. She was born about 1822 in Pennsylvania.

More About Daniel Delong:
Occupation: 1850 in Hocking Township, Fairfield County, Ohio; Plasterer

vii. Abraham Delong, son of Abraham Delong and Johannah Steman was born about 1821 in Ohio. He married Elizabeth Mowry on 26 Nov 1843 in Hocking County, Ohio. She was born about 1827 in Ohio. He married Catherine Mowry on 25 May 1854 in Hocking County, Ohio. She was born about 1825 in Ohio.

More About Abraham Delong:
Occupation: 1850 in Marion Township, Hocking County, Ohio; Farmer

viii. Anna Magdalena Delong, daughter of Abraham Delong and Johannah Steman was born in Apr 1823 in Ohio. She died on 25 Feb 1907 in Spencerville, Allen County, Ohio. She married Cornelius Stoneburner on 02 Mar 1843 in Fairfield County, Ohio. He was born about 1821 in Ohio. He died on 11 Feb 1895 in Spencer Township, Allen county, Ohio.

More About Cornelius Stoneburner:
Occupation: 1850 in Marion Township, Hocking County, Ohio; Farmer

ix. Hannah Delong, daughter of Abraham Delong and Johannah Steman was born on 29 Jun 1825 in Ohio. She died on 13 May 1886 in Logan Township, Auglaize County, Ohio. She married Joseph Pierson. He was born on 18 Nov 1826 in Fairfield County, Ohio. He died on 04 Mar 1900 in Logan Township, Auglaize County, Ohio.

More About Hannah Delong:
Burial: Allentown Cemetery, Allentown, Allen county, Ohio

Notes for Hannah Delong:
Birth date is from age at death on death record.

More About Joseph Pierson:
Burial: Allentown Cemetery, Allentown, Allen county, Ohio
Living In: 1860 Logan Township, Auglaize County, Ohio

Notes for Joseph Pierson:
Headstone has 73 years, 3 months and 16 days for age at death. Death record
has 73 years, 4 months and 14 days for age at death.
----

    x.   Isaac Delong, son of Abraham Delong and Johannah Steman was born about
1828 in Ohio. He died on 26 Apr 1899 in Crotty, Coffey County, Kansas. He
married Mary Ann Spohn on 26 Oct 1851 in Franklin County, Ohio. She was born
about 1829 in Ohio. He married Minerva A. Reed on 04 Jul 1888 in Coffey County,
Kansas. She was born about 1849.

More About Isaac Delong:
Burial: Big Creek Cemetery, Burlington, Coffey County, Kansas
Living In: 1850 Living with his parents in Marion Township, Hocking County,
Ohio.
Occupation: 1860 in Logan Township, Auglaize County, Ohio; Farmer
Occupation: 1870 in German Township, Allen County, Ohio; Farmer

More About Mary Ann Spohn:
Burial: Big Creek Cemetery, Burlington, Coffey County, Kansas

More About Isaac Delong and Mary Ann Spohn:
Marriage License: 25 Oct 1851 in Franklin County, Ohio

    xi.   Lydia Delong, daughter of Abraham Delong and Johannah Steman was born
about 1841 in Ohio.

Generation 8

158.   **Alexander Greenlee**. He married **Anna Henry**.

159.   **Anna Henry**.

Anna Henry and Alexander Greenlee had the following child:

79.   i.   Hannah Greenlee, daughter of Alexander Greenlee and Anna Henry was born on
26 Aug 1773. She died on 23 Feb 1865 in Mason County, West Virginia. She
married Edward Greenlee on 13 Jul 1792 in Virginia. He was born on 08 Sep
1761 in Ulster, Ireland. He died on 23 Aug 1839 in Mason County, Virginia.

248.   **Henry Delong**.

Henry Delong had the following child:

124.   i.   Abraham Delong, son of Henry Delong was born on 01 Jan 1773 in Pennsylvania. He
died on 03 Nov 1859 in Allen County, Ohio. He married Johannah Steman,

daughter of Christian Steman and Hannah Barr in Fayette County, Pennsylvania.
She was born on 10 May 1788 in Rockingham County, Virginia. She died in 1875
in Allen County, Ohio.

250. **Christian Steman**. He married **Hannah Barr**.

251. **Hannah Barr**.

Hannah Barr and Christian Steman had the following child:

125.   i. Johannah Steman, daughter of Christian Steman and Hannah Barr was born on 10 May
             1788 in Rockingham County, Virginia. She died in 1875 in Allen County, Ohio. She
             married Abraham Delong, son of Henry Delong in Fayette County, Pennsylvania. He
             was born on 01 Jan 1773 in Pennsylvania. He died on 03 Nov 1859 in Allen County,
             Ohio.

9 781979 834971